# POP GOES THE WEASEL

## The Secret Meanings of Nursery Rhymes

### ALBERT JACK

*Illustrated by Lara Carlini*

PENGUIN BOOKS

PENGUIN BOOKS

Published by the Penguin Group
Penguin Books Ltd, 80 Strand, London WC2R ORL, England
Penguin Group (USA) Inc., 375 Hudson Street, New York, New York 10014, USA
Penguin Group (Canada), 90 Eglinton Avenue East, Suite 700, Toronto, Ontario, Canada M4P 2Y3
(a division of Pearson Penguin Canada Inc.)
Penguin Ireland, 25 St Stephen's Green, Dublin 2, Ireland (a division of Penguin Books Ltd)
Penguin Group (Australia), 250 Camberwell Road, Camberwell, Victoria 3124, Australia
(a division of Pearson Australia Group Pty Ltd)
Penguin Books India Pvt Ltd, 11 Community Centre, Panchsheel Park, New Delhi – 110 017, India
Penguin Group (NZ), 67 Apollo Drive, Rosedale, North Shore 0632, New Zealand
(a division of Pearson New Zealand Ltd)
Penguin Books (South Africa) (Pty) Ltd, 24 Sturdee Avenue, Rosebank, Johannesburg 2196, South Africa

Penguin Books Ltd, Registered Offices: 80 Strand, London WC2R ORL, England

www.penguin.com

First published by Allen Lane 2008
Published in Penguin Books 2010
009

Albert Jack supports the MacKinnon Trust, a registered charity working to raise public awareness about
mental health issues such as schizophrenia and the care needed by those who suffer and their families,
*www.mackinnontrust.org*

The moral right of the author has been asserted

Printed in England by Clays Ltd, St Ives plc

978-0-141-03098-2

www.greenpenguin.co.uk

*This book is dedicated to my mum in Guildford, Sheila Podmore, because every mum should have a book dedicated to her at least once in her life. In fact, let me do it for you. This book is dedicated to your mum, too:*

.......................................
(insert name here)

# Contents

## Traditional Songs and Anthems

# Introduction

I first had the idea of studying the history of nursery rhymes about ten years ago. But at the time, the idea of trawling through history to discover the origins of our favourite nursery rhymes and analyse their meanings, obvious or hidden, was one I didn't altogether relish, to be honest. After all, what could possibly be interesting about a short, fat boy called Humpty or Dumpty, who lived a long, long time ago and who fell off his wall? Or, for that matter, how much fun can you have with three blind mice being chased around the kitchen by a farmer's wife? Surely that has happened on farms across the land since knives were first hacked out of flint? And why would anybody, in this case me, want to create a book full of stories such as the one about Jack Horner, a little boy who shoved his thumb into a pie and stole a plum? What drama is there in that? Even I have done a spot of plum-stealing from pies, and I wasn't a bad lad either.

But, instead, this has turned out to be the most rewarding piece of work I have done so far. Because once it becomes obvious that many nursery rhymes have been written about, or evolved from, particular historic events and then used as a means of passing important news around the countryside, simply by word of mouth, then the research becomes a fascinating study into a bygone way of life. For example, would you have expected **Humpty Dumpty** to be the name of one of King Charles I's cannons located on top of a church tower at the Siege of Colchester in 1648 during the English Civil War? Operated by One-Eyed Thompson, a Royalist gunner, it successfully kept Cromwell's forces at bay until the Parliamentarians managed to blow it off the tower, allowing them to take over the town. An important battle was lost (or won, depending on your viewpoint) and a turning point in history then marked by a rhyme, soon repeated in every village and every hamlet as news of the Roundheads' victory spread throughout the land.

Or would you imagine for a moment that the **three blind mice** could be the Oxford Martyrs Latimer, Ridley and Cranmer, all burned at the stake for their faith, by the **Farmer's Wife**, Mary I? Or what about who little Jack Horner really was, my personal favourite – the story of the steward to the Dean of Glastonbury, Thomas Horner, who was sent to see Henry VIII with a bowl full of property deeds disguised as a pie in an attempt to bribe the king? On the way to London, Horner, it is said, reached into the pie and a stole a **plum** piece of real estate for himself – a place called Mells Manor. And while some of the other stories behind the rhymes may well have been elaborated, embellished or even rewritten to suit events, in the case of 'Little Jack Horner' there really was a Thomas Horner at Glastonbury who took ownership of Mells Manor during the reign of Henry VIII and whose descendants still live there to this day. All in all, these so-called 'nursery' rhymes aren't the innocent little songs for children they purport to be!

The research was the best part of the process as it introduced me to such figures as the sixteenth-century spider
expert Dr Thomas Muffet and his daughter, **Little Miss
Muffet**, or Henry VIII's right-hand man Cardinal Wolsey,
the likeliest candidate for **Old Mother Hubbard**. Not
many of us have the chance to write about two such different individuals in the same week. The following week, a
savvy London prostitute, **Lucy Locket**, made her appearance, accompanied by Prince Frederick (son of 'mad' king
George III), the **Grand Old Duke of York** and blundering
military commander who disastrously **marched his men to
the top of the hill**, at Toucoing in northern France, where
they were soundly defeated. The week after that, I was
visiting some wonderful old London churches for the origins of 'Oranges and Lemons' and becoming acquainted
with the dark schemers who helped Richard III to power
and whose careers may have inspired 'Hey Diddle Diddle'.

The historical significance of children's rhymes is often
lost on most adults, let alone the children who learn them
by heart almost as soon as they learn to say anything at all.
For all of us, the first things we are taught, after learning
how to talk, are nursery rhymes. Hence by the time we are
adults, we will know the words to hundreds of them without ever being aware of their meaning or real importance.
And they are important, in my view, because many of them
tell the true tale of some of history's darkest or most tragic
events. Knowing the origins of a rhyme will help to preserve
that piece of history, or the layers of stories that accrue
around a centuries-old verse. It also provides a fascinating

insight into how news of historical events was transmitted around the land long before the days of instant communication by telephone, radio, television or the internet.

The name forever associated with English nursery rhymes is 'Mother Goose', conjuring an image of a cheerful, well-upholstered countrywoman who makes up rhymes to entertain her large brood of equally cheerful children. The term, associated with no specific writer and current since the seventeenth century, became widespread largely thanks to a French book of fairy tales by Charles Perrault. Published in 1697 and best known by its subtitle, *Contes de ma mère l'Oye* ('Tales of Mother Goose'), it was first translated into English in 1729, bringing to English readers the perennially popular tales of 'Little Red Riding Hood', 'Sleeping Beauty', 'Cinderella' and 'Puss in Boots'. But it wasn't until John Newbery produced a collection of rhymes called *Mother Goose Melody* in 1765 that 'Mother Goose' became inextricably linked with nursery rhymes. Newbery's collection was hugely popular, helping to establish an indelible place for such rhymes in the hearts and minds of the British people.

As for proving the origins of each rhyme, I have searched high and low, near and far, in an attempt to root out the definitive answer – or as near definitive as possible. Sometimes I have agreed with previous researchers and at other times feel they may have missed vital information, but, by and large, where I have arrived at two or more possible conclusions I have presented every option, leaving it to the reader to make up his or her mind. After all, this book has not been written to start arguments in the pub about nursery rhymes. It is simply meant to be a bit of fun and give you something to talk about with friends and family. And hopefully buy for distant relatives at Christmas.

In the process of researching the rhymes, I looked into the origins of a few of our traditional songs – including ones from across the Pond. So, while not being nursery rhymes as such, I have included their origins anyway, chiefly because they interested me and because I am sure they will interest you too. Indeed, you will now be able to tell your American friends how their revered national anthem began life as a drinking song from a London dockside pub.

Along the way, I have learned some wonderful stories, but I have also suffered personally for this book and made some mistakes I can help you avoid. For instance, I began researching the origins of 'Little Blue Betty' (I was sure that it must have something to do with Queen Elizabeth I) through the tried and tested medium of libraries and book-shops, but found myself getting nowhere. So one day I had a go on the internet instead, but when my girlfriend later checked the browser history, she promptly packed her bags. Such are the sacrifices I have made for you, dear reader. The least you can do now is join me on a journey through history to make sense of the rhymes we have all been enjoying since we first learned how to communicate without pointing and shouting.

Albert Jack
Cape Town
May 2008

# Acknowledgements

Special thanks to Peter Gordon. Once again, there is a good reason for it, but I can't tell you what it is. This time it would only embarrass me. To my sister Julie Willmott (she knows why), to Margeaux Dawe, little Reef, Paul and Gen Ryan, and Tony and Sheila Podmore.

Big thanks also to Paul March at Clintons in London and John Silbersack of the Trident Media Group in New York. Also to Nigel Harland, Caroline Harland and Tammy Green. To Lara Carlini for the fantastic illustrations and to Lisa Uga Carlini-Vidulin and Mel Roux in Cape Town.

The Penguin team must also receive huge credit for all the effort and hard work. And that's my editor Georgina Laycock, publicist Thi Dinh, designer Lisa Simmonds, cover designer Richard Green, as well as Ruth Stimson, Alice Dawson, Ruth Pinkney and Taryn Jones, without whom the book would not have got out on time. And a special thank you to Kate Parker, my copy editor.

Finally, to all the people working in bookshops across the world. I have a feeling that there will be good times ahead despite the credit crunch. I am sure people will be buying more books for each other this year, as most of the CDs I hear these days are rubbish and DVDs too expensive. So let's be positive and banish the blues by exercising the grey matter. After all, as you'll soon see from the evidence of these nursery rhymes and songs, they had things far tougher in 'the Good Old Days' ...

# NURSERY
# RHYMES

# An Apple a Day

AN apple a day keeps the doctor away.
Apple in the morning, doctor's warning.
Roast apple at night, starves the doctor outright.
Eat an apple at bed, knock the doctor on the head.
Three each day, seven days a week, ruddy apple,
     ruddy cheek.

The most surprising thing about this rhyme is that it wasn't invented by the apple industry, or even the association of greengrocers, if there is such a thing. It evolved during the sixteenth century and has been used ever since (sometimes rather desperately) as part of parental propaganda to get children to eat their greens. But what's interesting is the deep distrust of doctors and medical science it shows. Its advice is that doctors are to be avoided at all costs; they are only looking to make money out of you. Folk medicine (what we'd now call herbalism) was at odds with official medicine and often prescribed remedies that mirrored the result you'd be looking for. If you want a rosy, **ruddy** face then eat an apple; a red one, that is – green cheeks might necessitate a visit from the doctor after all.

# As I Was Going by Charing Cross

AS I was going by Charing Cross
I saw a black man upon a black horse;
They told me it was King Charles the First,
Oh dear, my heart was ready to burst.

This rhyme (with its echo of RIDE A COCK HORSE TO BANBURY CROSS) refers to the public execution of **King Charles** I on 30 January 1649 outside the palace of Whitehall, very close to **Charing Cross**. Following his capture and imprisonment by the Parliamentarians towards the end of the Civil War, Charles presented a huge problem to his captors. Alive, he posed a constant threat to their new state; dead, he would instantly become a hero. Eventually and reluctantly, they brought him to trial.

The lack of public support for the trial was painfully obvious, despite the harsh wording of the charge brought against him: 'Out of a wicked design to erect and uphold himself with an unlimited and tyrannical power to rule according to his own will and to overthrow the rights and the liberties of the people of England.' Showing the same arrogance that had brought on the Civil War, Charles refused even to answer the charge, believing that his own authority to rule had been given to him by God when he had been crowned and anointed, while the power wielded by those wishing to try him was simply that which grew out of a barrel of gunpowder. The court argued that no man was above the law, but when the king was duly found guilty, Richard Brandon, Hangman of London, summed up the general mood by refusing to carry out the task.

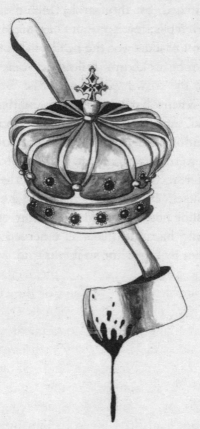

Eventually a man was paid £100, a ridiculous amount of money for the time, to act as executioner, but he insisted on remaining anonymous.

The killing of a king was hugely contentious, and the murder of the man divinely chosen to rule made the perfect ghoulish subject for a nursery rhyme. Although the execution was watched by thousands, including the famous diarist Samuel Pepys, few accounts of it survive to this day. It was common practice for the head of a person convicted of treason to be held up, following their decapitation, and shown to the crowd with the words: 'Behold the head of a traitor!' When Charles's head was exhibited, the words were not used, and unlike the carnival atmosphere at any normal execution, the mood of the crowd was sombre. Hearts really were **ready to burst**. Various strange phenomena were later recorded in relation to the execution: a beached whale at Dover died within an hour of Charles himself; a falling star appeared that night over Whitehall; and a man who had said the king deserved to die had his eyes pecked out by crows, or so it was said.

# As I Was Going to St Ives

AS I was going to St Ives,
I met a man with seven wives,
And every wife had seven sacks,
And every sack had seven cats,
And every cat had seven kits;
Kits, cats, sacks, wives,
How many were going to St Ives?

Another popular riddle posing as a nursery rhyme (see also FLOUR OF ENGLAND and IN MARBLE WALLS AS WHITE AS MILK), this one sets out to remind children that commonsense is even more valuable than applied mathematics. Although the earliest version of the rhyme was published in 1730, a similar riddle appears in the Rhind Mathematical Papyrus, dating from around 1650 BC. On hearing the riddle, many have fallen into the obvious trap – insisting that the answer is found by multiplying the number seven. The repetition of seven, a magical number in many cultures (see SOLOMON GRUNDY), seems to emphasize this, **seven wives, seven sacks, seven cats** and **seven kittens** multiplied together equalling 2,401, not including the **man** accompanying them all. But in fact the answer is one – the narrator himself. Because if you were going to St Ives and met all these people on your way, then presumably they are all coming back from St Ives, not going there. There's also a clue in the name **Ives** –'I' ('I've') or 'Me'.

# Baa, Baa, Black Sheep

BAA, baa, black sheep,
Have you any wool?
Yes, sir, yes, sir,
Three bags full;
One for the master,
One for the dame,
And one for the little boy
Who lives down the lane.

Some researchers believe this rhyme was written simply to encourage young children to imitate the sounds of animals when they are learning how to talk. But there's a far more interesting and historic background to the poem. The version we all grew up with was in fact altered to make it more pleasant for young ears. The poem had a different last line until at least 1765, when it was included in *Mother Goose Melody*, published by John Newbery. The last line originally went like this: 'And none for the little boy who cries in the lane.'

The surprising story behind this rhyme starts, unsurprisingly enough, with sheep. Sheep have been extremely valuable to the English economy for well over a thousand years. The wool trade in England was already thriving by August 1086 when the Domesday Book recorded that many flocks across the country numbered more than two thousand sheep. By the late twelfth century, sheep farming was big business and towns such as Guildford, Northampton, Lincoln and York had become thriving centres of production. By 1260, some flocks consisted of as many as

seven or eight thousand sheep, each tended by a dozen full-time shepherds, and English wool was regarded as the best in the world. But as the cloth workers of Belgium and France were far more skilled than the English at producing the finished article, much of the wool produced was exported to Europe where the raw material was dyed and woven into high-quality cloth.

When Edward I (the Plantagenet king also known as 'Longshanks' – see DOCTOR FOSTER) returned from his crusading in 1272 to be crowned king, he set about the type of reforms his father, Henry III, had been unable to achieve.

England had a growing number of wealthy wool merchants, chiefly in the form of the monasteries, and, thanks to the quality and reliability of English wool, an increasing number of eager buyers in the Italians and the Flemish, who dominated European business at the time. Naturally this also led to a growing number of traders and exporters and a great deal of money flowing into England on a regular basis. This, in turn, meant Edward was able to impose new taxes on the exports of wool to fund his military campaigns and keep the royal coffers topped up. In 1275, the Great Custom was introduced in the shape of a royal tax of six shillings and eight pence per wool sack – approximately one-third of the price of each sack. It was this wool tax that is said to be the basis of 'Baa, Baa, Black Sheep': one-third of the price of each sack must go to the king (the **master**), two-thirds to the Church or the monasteries (the **dame**), and none to the

Note: The **black sheep** of the family is generally regarded as a disgrace, different from the other members and with a rogue element implied. For thousands of years, a black lamb in a flock was always the unpopular one as its fleece could not be dyed and was therefore less valuable than those of the white lambs. It would therefore have been regarded as an unlucky omen, its presence disruptive to the rest of the flock. Thomas Bastard (yes, his real name) wrote a poem, published in 1598, in which he presents the black sheep as a predator: 'Till now I thought the proverbe did but jest, which said a black sheepe was a biting beaste.' And in 1892 Rudyard Kipling included in one of his own poems ('Gentleman-Rankers') the line 'We're little black sheep who've gone astray, Baa-aa-aa!', recalling both the rhyme and the proverbial waywardness of its woolly subject.

actual shepherd (**the little boy who cries in the lane**). Rather than being a gentle song about sharing things out fairly, it's a bitter reflection on how unfair things have always been for working folk throughout history.

During this period of great success (for the ruling classes at any rate), England's export of wool nearly doubled from 24,000 sacks to 47,000 sacks per year, and the money raised largely funded the Hundred Years' War with the French that dominated the fourteenth and fifteenth centuries. To this day, the Lord Speaker in the House of Lords (successor to the Lord Chancellor's role) sits on a sack made of wool, first introduced during the fourteenth century by the third consecutive Edward to rule England, Edward III.

## Bessy Bell and Mary Gray

BESSY Bell and Mary Gray,
They were two bonnie lasses:
They built their house upon the lea,
And covered it with rushes.

Bessy kept the garden gate
And Mary kept the pantry;
Bessy always had to wait,
While Mary lived in plenty.

It seems immediately obvious that the subjects of this rhyme must be history's best-known **Mary** and **Bessy** – Henry

VIII's two daughters, Mary and Elizabeth (Bessy). After Elizabeth's mother, Anne Boleyn, was executed in 1536, the two-year-old princess was declared illegitimate and sent away from court to live in the country. But she remained in constant danger, as she grew up, from her jealous elder sister, Mary. Once Mary had become queen in 1553, she even had 'Bessy' thrown into the Tower of London on trumped-up charges of treason. And so there she waited, by the **garden gate**, while Queen Mary lived in style. But the waiting was over three years later when, in 1558, Mary died and Elizabeth was finally able to claim the throne of England for herself.

However, there is another story behind this rhyme and it's not an English one. The version we know is in fact based on a rather longer Scottish ballad called 'The Twa Lasses'. Its opening verses tell a different tale:

> They theekit ower wi' rashes green,
> They theekit ower wi' heather;
> But the pest cam' frae the burrows-town,
> And slew them baith thegither.
> They thocht to lie in Methven kirk-yard,
> Amang their noble kin,
> But they maun lie in Dranoch-haugh
> To biek fornent the sun.

(There are many more verses, but you get the gist.) Meanwhile, the 1822 edition of *Archaeologia Scotica: Transactions of the Society of Antiquaries of Scotland* cites a letter written to John Swinton Esquire on 21 June 1781 by Major Augustine Barry of Lednock:

Dear Sir,
According to your desire, I have sent you the best account I can of Bessie Bell and Mary Gray.

When I first came to Lednock, I was shewn, in part of my ground (called the Dranoch-haugh), a heap of stones almost covered with briers, thorns and fern, which they assured me was the burial place of Bessie Bell and Mary Gray.

The tradition of the country relating to these ladies is that Mary Gray's father was laird of Lednock and Bessie Bell's of Kinvaid, a place in this neighbourhood. That they were both very handsome and an intimate friendship subsisted between them and that while Miss Bell was on a visit to Miss Gray the Plague broke out, in the year 1666. In order to avoid which they built themselves a bower about three quarters of a mile west from Lednock House, in a very retired and romantic place called Burnbraes, on the side of Beanchie-burn. Here they lived for some time, but the Plague raging with great fury, they caught the infection (it is said) from a young gentleman who was in love with them both. He used to bring them their provisions. They died in this bower and were buried in the Dranoch-haugh at the foot of a brae of the same name near to the bank of the river Almond. The burial place lies about half a mile west from the present house of Lednock.

> I have removed all the rubbish from this little spot of
> classic ground, enclosed it with a wall, planted it round
> with flowering shrubs, made up the grave double and fixed
> a stone in the wall on which are engraved the names of
> Bessie Bell and Mary Gray.

This account reflects the traditional tale told in the area, although the date of the events is more likely to be 1645 – when plague struck Perth and its environs, including Lednock. Interestingly, plague did not reach Scotland in either 1665 or 1666 thanks, mainly, to the Scots closing their borders and banning trade with London, effectively quarantining the entire country. Apart from that, there is nothing to say that the story doesn't have some basis in fact, and it remains widely believed. To this day, incurable romantics still make the pilgrimage to the grave, where they read the simple inscription: 'Bessie Bell and Mary Gray – They lived, they loved, they died'.

# The Big Ship Sails on the Ally-Ally-Oh

THE big ship sails on the ally-ally-oh,
The ally-ally-oh, the ally-ally-oh;
The big ship sails on the ally-ally-oh,
On the last day of September.

The captain said it will never, never do,
Never, never do, never, never do;
The captain said it will never, never do,
On the last day of September.

The big ship sank to the bottom of the sea,
The bottom of the sea, the bottom of the sea;
The big ship sank to the bottom of the sea,
On the last day of September.

We all dip our heads in the deep blue sea,
The deep blue sea, the deep blue sea;
We all dip our heads in the deep blue sea,
On the last day of September.

This rhyme, usually sung by children during skipping games, is thought to have been inspired by the building of the Manchester Ship Canal (hence 'alley' or **ally-ally-oh**), first used in 1894 to enable huge trading vessels (**big** ships) into the centre of Manchester via the port of Liverpool.

This created the unusual sight of massive steam ships pulling into the centre of a city far from the sea. The **last day of September** marks the end of the fair weather of summer and the start of the winter storms, which could spell disaster for any ship (**The big ship sank to the bottom of the sea**).

The final verse suggests a watery end for the crew of a shipwrecked vessel (**We all dip our heads in the deep blue sea**). Hence 'dipping' is most likely a euphemism for drowning, but it also has an echo of another kind of dipping – part of the ancient rituals of the communities who live and make their living by the sea. In Catholic countries, holy statues are still often carried down to the port on special days and dipped (along with the more enthusiastic worshippers) in the waves in order to seek protection against shipwreck and disaster in the year to come.

# The Blind Men and the Elephant

IT was six men of Indostan,
To learning much inclined,
Who went to see the Elephant,
Though all of them were blind,
That each by observation
Might satisfy his mind.

The First approached the Elephant,
And happening to fall
Against his broad and sturdy side,
At once began to bawl:
'Bless me, it seems the Elephant
Is very like a wall.'

The Second, feeling of the tusk,
Cried, 'Ho! What have we here,
So very round and smooth and sharp?
To me 'tis mighty clear
This wonder of an elephant
Is very like a spear.'

The Third approached the animal,
And happening to take
The squirming trunk within his hands,
Thus boldly up and spake:
'I see,' quoth he, 'the Elephant
Is very like a snake.'

The Fourth reached out an eager hand,
And felt about the knee.
'What most this wondrous beast is like
Is mighty plain,' quoth he;
''Tis clear enough the Elephant
Is very like a tree!'

The Fifth, who chanced to touch the ear,
Said, 'E'en the blindest man
Can tell what this resembles most;
Deny the fact who can,
This marvel of an Elephant
Is very like a fan.'

The Sixth no sooner had begun
About the beast to grope,
Than, seizing on the swinging tail
That fell within his scope;
'I see,' quoth he, 'the Elephant
Is very like a rope!'

And so these men of Indostan
Disputed loud and long,
Each in his own opinion
Exceeding stiff and strong,
Though each was partly in the right
And all were in the wrong.

*Moral:*

So oft in theologic wars
The disputants, I ween,
Rail on in utter ignorance
Of what each other means
And prate about an Elephant
Not one of them has seen.

'The Blind Men and the Elephant' was published in 1873 as part of a collection of rhymes and poems by John Godfrey Saxe. Saxe (1816–87) based his moral tale – more of a parable in the guise of a rhyme – upon a story of Indian origin that he called a 'Hindoo Fable'. It is probably quite ancient in origin, as similar tales are told in other religions, including Buddhism, Sufism, Islam and Jainism. In each, the number of blind men varies and sometimes they are not blind at all, but men in a darkened room with an elephant (clearly the only elephant in a room not to be ignored). The Hindu version of the tale goes something like this:

One day three blind men met, as usual, and sat under their favourite tree, talking about many things. All of a sudden, one of them said, 'I have heard that an elephant is a strange creature.' Another replied, 'Yes, it is too bad we are blind and do not have the good fortune to see this strange beast.' But the third said, 'Why do we need to see? Just to feel it would be wonderful.' At that moment, a passing merchant with a group of elephants came conveniently along and overheard their conversation. 'You fellows,' he called, 'if you really want to feel an elephant then come with me.' The three blind men were surprised but very happy. Taking each other by the hand, they quickly followed the merchant and began to speak excitedly about how the animal would feel and how they would form an image of it in their minds.

When they reached the elephants, the merchant told two of them to sit on the ground and wait while he led the first man to one of the beasts. With an outstretched arm, the man touched one of the elephant's front legs and then the other, stroking each from top to bottom. 'So,' he said, 'the strange animal is just like that.' Then the second man was led to the elephant. With an outstretched arm, he touched the creature on the trunk, stroking it up and down and from side to side. 'Ah, so now I know, I truly know!' he cried. The third man encountered the elephant's tail and wagged it from side to side. 'That's it,' he said, 'now I know too.'

The three blind men thanked the merchant and returned to their spot under the tree, each one excited about what he had learned. The first man said, 'This strange animal is just like two big trees without any branches.' Luckily, he was unable to see the expressions on his friends' faces, for they were horrified. 'No, no!' they cried in disbelief at what they had just heard. The second man then said, 'This animal is like a snake, long, strong and flexible.' 'What!' exclaimed the third man. 'You are both quite wrong. The elephant resembles a fly whisk, swishing from side to side.'

They argued about this for days, each insisting that he alone was correct, and of course – as Saxe points out in the conclusion to his rhyme – all three of them were **partly in the right / and all of them were wrong**. The moral is that nobody can claim to fully understand a subject until they have grasped – in this case, quite literally – the whole thing. Even then, it is never possible to know the full truth about something, simply because everyone, however knowledge-able or experienced, will view it in a different way. Hence, on a deeper level, the **elephant** can be seen as reality, and we are all the **blind men,** each of us able to perceive only a tiny part of a much greater whole.

# Bobby Shafto

> BOBBY Shafto's gone to sea,
> Silver buckles on his knee;
> He'll come back and marry me,
> Bonny Bobby Shafto!
> Bobby Shafto's bright and fair,
> Combing down his yellow hair;
> He's my love for evermair,
> Bonny Bobby Shafto!

Sung to the tune of an old sea shanty, this sounds much like a generic song sung by a sailor's sweetheart waiting for his return, but the real Robert Shafto had nothing to do with the sea or with keeping his promises. He was born into a political family in 1732 at Whitworth, near Spennymoor in County Durham. Both his father John and his uncle Robert were Members of Parliament and Robert the younger joined them in 1760 when he won the seat of County Durham. He held the seat until 1768 when he moved south and became the MP for Downton in Wiltshire. It was during his election campaigns that his supporters started calling him **Bonny Bobby Shafto** in an attempt to win public favour.

Robert Shafto may have achieved political success but he was apparently notorious for his bad treatment of the women in his life. The story behind the rhyme is believed to derive from the callous ending of his long engagement to Bridget Belasyse by his sudden marriage to another woman (wealthy heiress Anne Duncombe) on 18 April 1774, the eve of their proposed wedding. Legend has it that Bridget died of a broken heart just two weeks later.

Then, during his marriage to Anne, the previously penniless MP set about the task of spending his new wife's fortune, all the while courting various other young ladies with the promise of marriage. I guess you could see him as a Premiership footballer of his day leaving a wannabe WAG in every town. In the event, Bonny Bobby and Anne remained married until her death in July 1784. And Bobby Shafto never delivered on any of his wedding promises after that. He lived on until November 1797, just long enough to spend the rest of his wife's cash. His body is buried in the Shafto family crypt at Whitworth Church.

While there is little doubt Robert Shafto is the subject of the rhyme, recent research now suggests Bridget Belasyse actually died of tuberculosis on 6 April 1774, nearly two weeks before Shafto married Anne Duncombe. So perhaps he was the one left broken-hearted instead. Which cheers me up a little – although he was still pretty quick off the mark with Anne.

# Boys and Girls, Come Out to Play

BOYS and girls, come out to play,
The moon doth shine as bright as day;
Leave your supper, and leave your sleep
And come with your playfellows into the street.
Come with a whoop, come with a call,
Come with a good will or not at all.
Up the ladder and down the wall,
A half-penny loaf will serve us all;
You find milk, and I'll find flour,
And we'll have a pudding in half an hour.

This rhyme dates back to the beginning of the eighteenth century or earlier, to a time when children generally worked during the day and so could not play until the evening. It is believed that children, up until the nineteenth century, might sing such a rhyme to their playmates to come and join them outside. But there are slightly sinister overtones too. Night was the time of witches, fairies and evil spirits, after all, and the **moon** in particular was seen as intensifying their power or tempting forth even more dangerous creatures, such as werewolves.

This poem is a summons to children (the antithesis of WEE WILLIE WINKIE), to leave the safety of their homes and to come out and play – with their enticing magical playmates. But as any child who knew their fairy tales could tell you, fairy time passed at a completely different rate to normal time. One evening spent playing with your new companions and you could return home only to find that everyone you had known had died of old age. Maybe safer to stay in with the PlayStation, after all ...

# Christmas Is Coming

CHRISTMAS is coming, the goose is getting fat,
Please to put a penny in the old man's hat;
If you haven't got a penny, a halfpenny will do,
If you haven't got a halfpenny, a farthing will do,
If you haven't got a farthing, then God bless you!

The one enduring feature of Christmas since records began has been the desire to eat well at the festive season. The wealthy would indulge in huge, lavish banquets but they could do that at any time of year. For the majority of the population, Christmas was the one time when they could hope to have something special on the table, and whatever their circumstances, everyone tried hard to achieve some semblance of a feast. Although turkeys had been introduced to Britain during the 1700s, **goose** remained the traditional choice for a family Christmas dinner up until the twentieth century.

However, before the late twentieth century many people could not afford what others took for granted and were delighted to have any kind of meat on their table. The strong tradition of charity at Christmas therefore played an important role in providing something special for the poor family's dinner, especially in rural areas. Farmers often gave a bird or a joint of meat to their workers as a sort of Christmas bonus, and paternalistic squires provided meals for poor tenants and workhouse residents. As the rhyme shows, it was the one time of year that the poor and indigent could beg and confidently expect to be helped (**Please to put a penny in the old man's hat**).

Things were different in the towns and one very useful Victorian invention for the working family was the 'goose club' in which the members would pay a small sum every week to save up for their Christmas bird. The meetings of the goose clubs were parties in themselves. Although criticized by some reformers for encouraging people to drink, they served a very useful purpose and live on today in the form of the Christmas clubs set up by local shops and businesses.

Today turkey has overtaken goose as the centrepiece of the traditional festive dinner, but for the Victorians a goose was an integral part of Christmas feasting – most famously illustrated in Dickens's *A Christmas Carol* (1843) and making an appearance in a Sherlock Holmes story ('The Adventure of the Blue Carbuncle', 1892 – the stolen jewel being found in the bird's crop).

# The Cutty Wren

WE will go to the wood, says Robin to Bobbin,
We will go to the wood, says Richard to Robin,
We will go to the wood, says John all alone,
We will go to the wood, says everyone.

What to do there? says Robin to Bobbin,
What to do there? says Richard to Robin,
What to do there? says John all alone,
What to do there? says everyone.

We'll shoot at a wren, says Robin to Bobbin,
We'll shoot at a wren, says Richard to Robin,
We'll shoot at a wren, says John all alone,
We'll shoot at a wren, says everyone.

She's down, she's down, says Robin to Bobbin,
She's down, she's down, says Richard to Robin,
She's down, she's down, says John all alone,
She's down, she's down, says everyone.

Then pounce, then pounce, says Robin to Bobbin,
Then pounce, then pounce, says Richard to Robin,
Then pounce, then pounce, says John all alone,
Then pounce, then pounce, says everyone.

She is dead, she is dead, says Robin to Bobbin,
She is dead, she is dead, says Richard to Robin,
She is dead, she is dead, says John all alone,
She is dead, she is dead, says everyone.

In a cart with six horses, says Robin to Bobbin,
In a cart with six horses, says Richard to Robin,
In a cart with six horses, says John all alone,
In a cart with six horses, says everyone.

Then hoist, boys, hoist, says Robin to Bobbin,
Then hoist, boys, hoist, says Richard to Robin,
Then hoist, boys, hoist, says John all alone,
Then hoist, boys, hoist, says everyone.

How shall we dress her? says Robin to Bobbin,
How shall we dress her? says Richard to Robin,
How shall we dress her? says John all alone,
How shall we dress her? says everyone.

We'll hire seven cooks, says Robin to Bobbin,
We'll hire seven cooks, says Richard to Robin,
We'll hire seven cooks, says John all alone,
We'll hire seven cooks, says everyone.

How shall we boil her? says Robin to Bobbin,
How shall we boil her? says Richard to Robin,
How shall we boil her? says John all alone,
How shall we boil her? says everyone.

In the brewer's big pan, says Robin to Bobbin,
In the brewer's big pan, says Richard to Robin,
In the brewer's big pan, says John all alone,
In the brewer's big pan, says everyone.

'The Cutty Wren' – one of many rhymes written in a cumulative way (see FOR WANT OF A NAIL, THE HOUSE THAT JACK BUILT and WHO KILLED COCK ROBIN?) – derives from an ancient custom, once widespread throughout the British Isles. The tradition of hunting the wren was carried out on St Stephen's Day (26 December). The antiquary and writer John Aubrey (1626–97) tells of 'a whole Parish running like madmen from Hedge to Hedge a Wren-hunting'. Parties of men and boys killed one or more wrens (or pretended to do so), which they then placed in a garland-like 'bush' or special box and perambulated the village, singing, dancing, playing instruments and collecting money. The rhyme was chanted in the ceremonial procession after the kill had been made.

Part of the Boxing Day ritual seems to stem from this tiny bird being treated as if it were larger than an elephant. The wren, whose feathers were thought to provide protection against shipwreck, was regarded as the king of birds, due to an ancient folk tale. According to this, in a competition to see who should be king of the birds, the eagle flew higher and faster than all the others. Just as he was proclaiming his victory, the wren, who had hidden in his feathers, popped out and flew a few inches higher, claiming the crown.

# Ding, Dong, Bell

DING, dong, bell,
Pussy's in the well.
Who put her in?
Little Johnny Flynn.
Who pulled her out?
Little Tommy Stout.
What a naughty boy was that
To try to drown poor pussy cat,
Who never did him any harm,
And killed all the mice in his father's barn.

Tracing the origins of this nursery rhyme is relatively straightforward. It would have been composed as a cautionary tale for badly behaved children, to encourage them to be more compassionate – especially to defenceless animals. It is in a similar vein to other poems and rhymes with a moral message that were so popular in the eighteenth and nineteenth centuries (see LITTLE BO PEEP and MARY HAD A LITTLE LAMB).

However, the rhyme's echo of Shakespeare's famous song from *The Tempest* (1610), about a drowned sailor (rather than a drowned cat), has led some people to argue that the Bard himself may have written it:

> Full fathom five thy father lies ...
> Sea nymphs hourly ring his knell:
> Hark! now I hear them – Ding, dong, bell.

The refrain also appears in *The Merchant of Venice* (1596–8):

> Let us all ring fancy's knell;
> I'll begin – Ding, dong, bell.

Meanwhile, a contemporary rhyme goes:

> Jacke boy, ho boy newes,
> The cat is in the well,
> Let us ring now for her knell,
> Ding dong ding dong bell.

Appearing in 1609 in *Pammelia, Musickes Miscellanie*, this rhyme was therefore published after *The Merchant of Venice*, but further investigation shows that it in fact predates the play – going back to at least 1580. Which makes it look as though Shakespeare was simply quoting what was already a well-known rhyme. Ringing bells were clearly all the rage with the Elizabethans – or with Elizabethan poets, that is. One thing that all these related rhymes point to, is that the version we all know is a somewhat sanitized one – perhaps to avoid upsetting sensitive children. **Ding, dong, bell** is a knell, a bell rung to mark a death. Little Johnny Flynn had actually succeeded in drowning the **poor pussy cat**.

# Doctor Foster

DOCTOR Foster
Went to Gloucester
In a shower of rain.
He stepped in a puddle
Right up to his middle
And never went there again.

Like the last example, this rhyme would have been used as
a warning to children – this time that danger lurks around
every corner and that they should watch their step. Before
the days of tarmacadam, large potholes in the road were
common and could easily be mistaken for shallow puddles,
which, as we all know, attract children like a magnet.

One theory runs that the origins of this verse stretch back
over seven hundred years to Edward I (1239–1307), who
was known by the nickname of Doctor Foster – perhaps
because he was a learned fellow, or just someone in authority, from the Latin *doctor*, meaning a teacher or instructor.
One day, on a visit to Gloucester during a rainstorm, the
king rode his horse through what appeared to be a shallow
puddle. When it turned out to be a deep ditch, both king
and horse became trapped in the mud and had to be hauled
out by the good folk of Gloucester, much to Edward's fury
and embarrassment. The king, also known as 'Longshanks'
(if not quite long enough to negotiate deep puddles) or
'Edward the Lawgiver' and responsible for much of the

Tower of London in the form that we know it today, vowed never to return to Gloucester – and he remained true to his word.

However, another, rather more likely, theory concerns the geography of Gloucester itself. As Britain's most inland port, Gloucester is located on the banks of the River Severn – a low-lying area highly prone to flooding, as recent years have shown, and therefore with puddles aplenty. Relatively close to the Welsh border, the town would have been of strategic importance to Edward during his campaigns against the Welsh. Hence it is quite possible that 'Foster' follows 'Doctor' – the long-legged, learned, lawgiving king – simply because it rhymes with 'Gloucester'.

## Elsie Marley

> ELSIE Marley has grown so fine,
> She won't get up to feed the swine,
> But lies in bed until eight or nine,
> And surely she does take her time.

The protagonist of this rhyme, which was first written down in the mid eighteenth century, is believed by some to be Alice Marley, a North Country 'alewife' or landlady, who lived earlier in the century. An alternative, more satisfying theory is that Elsie is in fact 'Eppie', the heroine of a Scottish version of the rhyme:

Saw ye Eppie Marley, honey,
The woman that sells the barley, honey;
She's lost her pocket and all her money
By following Jacobite Charlie, honey.

Eppie Marley's turned so fine,
She'll no gang out to herd the swine,
But lies in her bed till eight or nine
And winna come down the stairs to dine.

The hidden meaning behind the seemingly innocent verse would have been well understood by the clansmen north of the border. Jacobite Charlie, better known as Bonnie Prince Charlie, was none other than Charles Edward Stuart (1720–88). Depending on which side of the border you hailed from, the so-called Young Pretender was either a Scottish terrorist or – as the grandson of James II, deposed in the Glorious Revolution of 1688 (see THE GRAND OLD DUKE OF YORK) – the rightful king of both England and Scotland.

In 1745, Bonnie Prince Charlie arrived in Scotland to lay claim to the thrones of Scotland, Ireland and England in opposition to King George II. Already a popular and romantic figure, Charlie was soon rallying support for his claim, and several rhymes and songs from that time encourage the good folk of Scotland to fight for their prince. But there were huge dangers inherent in such support, as the Scots were to learn after their defeat at the Battle of Culloden on 16 April 1746.

After the rout, the English under the command of the Duke of Cumberland were ordered that 'no quarter' be given to the Scots, which meant the wounded and captured were simply slaughtered on the battlefield to ensure they never rose against the English again. The Scottish economy was also deliberately devastated and morale was flattened for generations. Hence 'Eppie Marley' can be seen as a cautionary tale, warning children against any future association with the Stuarts. Like Charlie himself, who did not distinguish himself in the campaign, the supporters of the Stuarts are pictured as effeminate, seeing themselves as too **fine** to engage in day-to-day work like the rest of their community. (See also THE LION AND THE UNICORN and THE SKYE BOAT SONG for more on the effects of **Jacobite Charlie**.)

# Flour of England

FLOUR of England, fruit of Spain
Met together in a shower of rain;
Put in a bag and tied with a string;
If you tell me this riddle,
I'll give you a ring.

At first glance, this seems the world's strangest recipe for plum pudding. While that may be the obvious answer to the riddle the rhyme is asking, there could be rather more to it than that, however.

The origins of this rhyme, it is suggested, hark back to the Tudors and their relationship with Spain. Both Henry VIII and his daughter Mary were at one time married to members of the Spanish royal family. Neither union was a success: Henry's divorce from Catherine of Aragon is the subject of several nursery rhymes (see OLD MOTHER HUBBARD, SING A SONG OF SIXPENCE and THREE BLIND MICE); Mary's marriage, meanwhile, was part of a desperate campaign to reimpose Roman Catholicism on England and to prevent her younger sister, Elizabeth, from succeeding her and returning England to the Protestant faith.

The simplest way to do this was to produce an heir of her own, thereby blocking her sister's path to the throne, and this meant finding herself a husband. When Mary was shown a portrait of Prince Philip of Spain, she fell deeply in love on the spot. His father, the Holy Roman Emperor Charles V, agreed to send the prince to England and, legend has it, the two met for the first time in the pouring rain (**Flour of England, fruit of Spain / Met together in a shower of rain**). The following day, the queen publicly sent Philip a ring, signifying their engagement, and the pair were married the day after that. But, in the end, Mary died childless five years later, which may have had something to do with Philip's lack of 'carnal love' for her, by his own admission. Although I doubt he admitted it to Mary.

So that's one theory of the story behind this rhyme, but Elizabeth's reign brings with it a different interpretation. After Mary's death, Philip, now king of Spain and keen to keep his hold over the English throne, proposed to Elizabeth instead. But she managed to stall him for some years until it eventually became obvious that she had no intention of marrying him at all. This insult and her execution in 1587 of Mary, Queen of Scots, leaving no Catholic heir to the English throne, led to Philip's planned invasion of England. Luckily for Elizabeth, her admiral Lord Howard of Effingham and vice admiral Francis Drake (the 'flower' of England), with the indispensable help of a good English storm (**met together in a shower of rain**), managed to rout the vastly superior forces of Philip's Armada. The riddle of why they weren't able to win, despite overwhelmingly superior forces, was one that the Spanish were unable to answer. Hence the final line – **If you tell me this riddle, I'll give you a ring** – is an English taunt to the Spanish king, reminding him yet again that he would never again be king of England, either by marriage or by force.

## For Want of a Nail

FOR want of a nail the shoe was lost.
For want of a shoe the horse was lost.
For want of a horse the rider was lost.
For want of a rider the battle was lost.
For want of a battle the kingdom was lost.
And all for the want of a horseshoe nail.

The earliest known written version of a rhyme along the lines of 'For Want of a Nail' can be found in *Confessio*

*Amantis* ('The Lover's Confession'), a 33,000-line poem by John Gower (*c*.1330–1408), published between 1386 and 1390:

> For sparinge of a litel cost
> Ful ofte time a man hath lost
> The large cote for the hod [hood].

'For Want of a Nail' is a fine example of the sort of nursery rhyme written by teachers, probably in this case military men, to encourage others to think carefully about their actions and consider all possible consequences. In this case, the speaker is explaining, through a clever build-up of repeated phrases, each differing very slightly from the previous one, how a huge disaster could have been avoided by a small, thoughtful action only a few stages earlier. The lesson is that the entire kingdom could be lost to an enemy army if small tasks such as nailing a horseshoe correctly are not carried out properly. As the Boy Scouts say, 'Be prepared.'

These days, the rhyme could be seen as a version of the Butterfly Effect – how mathematicians illustrate Chaos Theory by suggesting how some tiny, seemingly insignificant action, such as a butterfly flapping its wings in one part of the world, can, in principle, trigger a series of escalating events that could result in a devastating tornado somewhere else.

Getting back to that ill-fitting horseshoe, it appears that in days gone by most English kings didn't court chaos but prepared particularly thoroughly for battle, taking few chances when it came to equipment and training. As early as 1252, the Assize of Arms ordered that all men aged between fifteen and sixty-five must be 'equipped with a bow and arrows' and that those in possession of between 40 and 100 shillings should also own a dagger and sword. In 1363, King Edward III ordered archery practice to be compulsory for all non-military citizens on a Sunday and every public holiday, giving rise to the great archery contests of the Middle Ages.

The skill of English archers became celebrated. Indeed, legend has it that the famous two-fingered V-sign evolved from the gestures of archers fighting at the Battle of Agincourt in 1415. The myth claims that when the French captured English archers, they cut off the two fingers used to pull back the bowstring to ensure they could no longer use their bows against them. As a result, those who had not been handicapped in this way would show their defiance by waving two fingers to their enemy, illustrating they were still capable of beating them.

## Frère Jacques

FRÈRE Jacques, Frère Jacques,
Dormez-vous, dormez-vous?
Sonnez les matines, sonnez les matines!
Din, din, don, din, din, don.

*Translated as:*

BROTHER John, Brother John,
Are you sleeping, are you sleeping?
Ring the morning bells, ring the morning bells!
Ding, dang, dong, ding, dang, dong.

Usually sung as a round (see also LONDON'S BURNING and TURN AGAIN, WHITTINGTON), this is one French song every English-speaking schoolchild knows. Rather than somebody's lazy brother having a lie-in, **Frère Jacques** is generally held to be a monk, being called to ring the bells for matins or morning prayer (**sonnez les matines**). There are a number of potential candidates for him.

Some believe Friar Jacques could be Jacques de Molay (1249–1314), the twenty-third (and final) Grand Master of the very powerful Knights Templar. When sentenced to life imprisonment by Pope Clement V, de Molay, not knowing when to keep his head down, furiously challenged the Pope before God and so was burned at the stake.

Others have suggested the inspiration for the rhyme is Frère Jacques Beaulieu (1651–1720), a Dominican friar known for pioneering gallstone surgery, usually with disastrous results, or Jacques Clément (1567–89), another Dominican, who became famous – or rather, infamous – for assassinating the French king Henri III. Clément had gained access to the king by saying that he carried an important private message. In what was clearly an early suicide mission, he stabbed Henri in the chest and was immediately killed himself by the king's guard. Henri died the following day from his wounds.

But frankly, it's much more likely that the song was intended to mock monks in general, who seemed, to lay observers, (take Chaucer's *Canterbury Tales* for example) as though they never did or said anything of any note and contributed nothing to society, just taking their ease and ringing the odd bell.

# A Frog He Would
# A-Wooing Go

A FROG he would a-wooing go,
Hey ho! says Rowley,
Whether his mother would let him or no;
With a rowley, powley, gammon and spinach,
Hey ho! says Anthony Rowley.

So off he set with his opera hat,
Hey ho! says Rowley,
And on the road he met with a rat;
With a rowley, powley, gammon and spinach,
Hey ho! says Anthony Rowley.

They came to the door of Mousey's hall,
Hey ho! says Rowley,
They gave a loud knock, and they gave a loud call;
With a rowley, powley, gammon and spinach,
Hey ho! says Anthony Rowley.

Pray, Mrs Mouse, will you give us some beer?
Hey ho! says Rowley,
For Froggy and I are fond of good cheer;
With a rowley, powley, gammon and spinach,
Hey ho! says Anthony Rowley.

But while they were all a-merry-making,
Hey ho! says Rowley,
A cat and her kittens came tumbling in;
With a rowley, powley, gammon and spinach,
Hey ho! says Anthony Rowley.

The cat she seized the rat by the crown,
Hey ho! says Rowley,
The kittens they pulled the little mouse down;
With a rowley, powley, gammon and spinach,
Hey ho! says Anthony Rowley.

This put Mr Frog in a terrible fright,
Hey ho! says Rowley,
He took up his hat and wished them goodnight;
With a rowley, powley, gammon and spinach,
Hey ho! says Anthony Rowley.

But as Froggy was crossing over a brook,
Hey ho! says Rowley,
A lily-white duck came and gobbled him up;
With a rowley, powley, gammon and spinach,
Hey ho! says Anthony Rowley.

So there was the end of one, two, three,
Hey ho! says Rowley,
The rat, the mouse and the little frog-ee;
With a rowley, powley, gammon and spinach,
Hey ho! says Anthony Rowley.

This is a song that has changed over the centuries to reflect the times. The first known version of it, published in 1549, has been found under the title 'The Frog Came to the Myl Dur' in Robert Wedderburn's *Complaynt of Scotland*. In 1547, under attack from the English king Henry VIII, the Scottish queen consort, Mary of Guise, turned to her allies in France for assistance. The French obliged and Henri II (of France) then proposed to unite their two countries against the English by marrying his three-year-old son Louis (the **frog**) to her daughter Princess Mary (**Mrs Mouse**), the future Queen of Scots. It is this engagement that is thought to be behind the original version of 'A Frog He Would A-Wooing Go'. The song proved unfortunately prophetic: Louis did not long survive their wedding thirteen years later.

The song re-emerged in England some years later when another example of French wooing caused some concern. This time it was the long courtship between Elizabeth I and the Duke of Anjou in 1579. Despite the twenty-one-year age gap between them, Elizabeth liked the young duke best of all her many suitors, affectionately nicknaming Anjou 'her **frog**' and bestowing many gifts upon him. But there was real alarm among the English people, including most of the queen's own Privy Council, at how well **Mousey** was getting on with the French Catholic, and eventually, after much consultation with her advisers, the Queen reluctantly sent her young beau on his way.

But the story behind the version we all know today is rather different. The refrain **Hey ho! says Anthony Rowley** was added over a century later, while the **frog** the rhyme refers to is an English rather than a French king: Charles II.

After his father's defeat at the hands of Cromwell (see As I Was Going by Charing Cross and There Was a Crooked Man), the prince had spent years on the continent at various European courts. By the time of the Restoration in 1660, he cut a raffish, exotic figure in an England starved of colour and frivolity. Cromwell had banned every form of merry-making, from dancing to Christmas, and Charles, determined to enjoy himself as much as possible, cancelled all these new laws. His court soon became notorious for its love of pleasure, while at the forefront of every new craze, from horse racing to high fashion, was the king.

But it was for his wooing that the king was best known. He was called 'Old Rowley' by his subjects after his famous stallion of that name – to quote Dennis Wheatley: 'owing to the obvious similarity of their masculine vigour'. A portion of the Newmarket racecourse is still called the Rowley Mile, after the celebrated animal. Charles openly kept many mistresses: most notably Nell Gwyn, Louise de Kéroualle and Barbara Palmer, the Countess of Castlemaine, although there were many more. He openly acknowledged at least fourteen illegitimate children, by several different mothers, but he had no children with his wife, Catherine of Braganza. It is thought that the two aggressors who wanted to eat **Anthony Rowley** up were his two favourites: **the cat** was the very ambitious Castlemaine – **her kittens** being her five royal bastards – and the **lily-white duck** Nell Gwyn. In the case of Castlemaine, Charles managed to escape her toils – eventually banishing her from court for her promiscuity and for making too free with the Privy Purse – but it was 'pretty, witty Nell' who remained true to him and she ended up with the prize: the love of the king (**A lily-white duck came and gobbled him up**). On his deathbed in 1685, the king famously begged his brother and successor, James: 'Do not let poor Nelly starve.'

## Georgie Porgie

GEORGIE Porgie, pudding and pie,
Kissed the girls and made them cry;
When the boys came out to play,
Georgie Porgie ran away.

There is a sinister undertone to this nursery rhyme; Georgie Porgie really seems to be up to no good, otherwise the girls would not be crying and he would not have to run away when the boys came out to play. So what is it all about, then?

There are two Georges whose stories fit the events. One was George Villiers (1592–1628), the handsome son of an insignificant nobleman but who soon climbed his own way into the court of James I and the king's favour. Aged just twenty-three, he was given the somewhat unnerving position of Gentleman of the Bedchamber.

Rumour had it that he and the king were more than good friends. It certainly would explain why within two years he had been made an earl and then a marquess. Five years later, aged just thirty-one, George became the 1st Duke of Buckingham, proving quite clearly that the king's bed-chamber was the place to be for any aspiring nobleman in the early seventeenth century.

The nursery rhyme is said to mock both James I and George Villiers over their open romantic interest in each other. In fact, the king even proclaimed to the Privy Council that 'you may be sure that I love the Duke of Buckingham more than anybody else and I wish not to have it thought to be a defect'. Although the king once announced that homosexuality was among the crimes that 'we are bound in conscience never to forgive', it is now believed by historians studying court diaries and correspondence that the pair were indeed lovers. The king even called Georgie 'my sweet child and wife' as if to emphasize the point.

But George Villiers was also known to be partial to both sexes and had many affairs with both the young ladies of court and the wives and daughters of other powerful Englishmen, causing resentment all around, although his relationship with the king gave him a certain amount of immunity. It had also been whispered that he often took advantage of his privileged position and forced his affections upon the said ladies, causing outrage (**Kissed the girls and made them cry**) while managing to avoid confrontation or retaliation (**When the boys came out to play, / Georgie Porgie ran away**).

George Villiers's luck eventually ran out when, in 1627, he became embroiled in military matters and led an unsuccessful campaign on behalf of James's son, Charles I, during which the former rent-boy-made-good accidentally lost over four thousand men out of an army of seven thousand. On his return to Portsmouth, he was stabbed to death by one of the wounded soldiers, furious at his commander's lack of military judgement and the loss of so many of his English comrades. 'Georgie Porgie' was laid to rest at Westminster Abbey later that year.

Another candidate for the real Georgie Porgie is the

Prince Regent George IV, the hapless son, with half an inch of brain, of mad King George III (see THE GRAND OLD DUKE OF YORK). Immensely fat (**Georgie Porgie, pudding and pie**), his corset-wearing was the source of constant ridicule and satirical cartoons. By 1797, his weight had reached seventeen and a half stone and by 1824 his corsets were being made for a waist of fifty inches.

This George was unquestionably heterosexual but he took as much advantage of his position as George Villiers had done. He had a roving eye: attractive female visitors to the parties he gave at the Pavilion in Brighton were often advised to avoid being left alone with him. His chequered love life involved several mistresses, illegitimate children and even bigamy. He had an official wife, Caroline of Brunswick, whom he detested so much he even banned her from his coronation, and an unofficial one – Maria Anne Fitzherbert (as she was both a Catholic and a commoner, their marriage was not formally recognized and remained a secret) – and he managed to make both women miserable (**Kissed the girls and made them cry**).

In addition, although George loved watching prizefighting (bare-knuckle boxing), which at that time was illegal, his own physical and emotional cowardice was legendary. This is illustrated by a story of the most infamous prizefight of the day, where one contestant died of his injuries. George was known to have been present, as he was included in a sketch of the match by James Gillray (the famous political cartoonist), but when the man died he ran away, terrified of being implicated in the fallout and attempting to conceal his

presence at the match (**When the boys come out to play, /
Georgie Porgie ran away**).

# Good King Arthur

WHEN good King Arthur ruled this land,
He was a goodly king;
He stole three packs of barley meal
To make a bag of pudding.

A bag of pudding the king did make,
And stuffed it well with plums,
And in it put great lumps of fat,
As big as my two thumbs.

The king and queen did eat thereof,
And noblemen beside;
And what they could not eat that night,
The Queen next morning fried.

King Arthur is a fabled British leader, said in medieval tales
and chronicles to have ruled over England and defended
it against Saxon invaders following the withdrawal of the
Romans in the fifth century. But at the start of the Dark
Ages, when the island was under constant threat of invasion, and at various other troubled moments in their history,
the inhabitants of Britain longed for a strong leader who
could unite their fragmented regions under one rule and

enable them to defend themselves. Hence the legend of King Arthur, the saviour king, was hugely appealing, its popularity spreading over the years, thanks especially to Geoffrey of Monmouth's *Historia Regnum Britanniae* ('History of the Kings of England'), written in about 1136, and to Thomas Malory's *Le Morte d'Arthur*, published in 1485.

Largely thanks to Malory, the legend of King Arthur was integral to the medieval conception of English history, but with the waning of the Middle Ages came a lessening of belief in the story. While the stories continued to be popular, their truth was disputed. The sixteenth-century humanist scholar Polydore Vergil famously rejected the idea of a post-Roman Arthurian empire, calling it a fabrication – much to the horror of Welsh and English antiquarians.

This nursery rhyme, with its down-to-earth king and queen, would seem to stem from this period. After all, far from being a heroic figure of high chivalry – as portrayed by Malory – this **goodly king** is now a thief. Arthur's famous banquets, where no one could eat until a marvel had occurred (from headless knights and damsels in distress to visions of the Holy Grail), have turned into a slapstick pudding-making and -eating session. Guinevere, rather than being the mysterious, beautiful queen and object of forbidden love, is demoted to a penny-pinching housewife, thriftily frying up the remains of the pudding for breakfast. It's hard not to feel that the author of the rhyme must have heard the Arthurian legends one time too many. Opening with **When good King Arthur ruled this land,** this rhyme mocks both the high-flown poetry of *Le Morte d'Arthur* and wistfulness for ye goode olde days that almost certainly never were.

## Goosie, Goosie Gander

GOOSIE, goosie gander,
Whither shall I wander?
Upstairs, downstairs
And in my lady's chamber.
There I met an old man
Who wouldn't say his prayers;
I took him by the left leg
And threw him down the stairs.

The origins of this rhyme are believed to date back to sixteenth-century England and the Papist purge. Many noble families, particularly in the north, became publicly Protestant but remained privately Catholic. This was treason because Queen Elizabeth was head of the Protestant Church of England and Roman Catholicism was outlawed. Most manor houses had their own private chapels, and priests would often be smuggled in to conduct services. It was a very dangerous business as everyone caught would be certain of the severest penalties. But since, for a committed Catholic, not christening your new baby or dying unconfessed and without last rites was to pretty much guarantee eternal damnation, many thought it worth the risk.

**Goosie gander** represents the priest. Like the Catholic

Church, geese have traditionally been associated with Rome – in fact, ever since the honking of the geese at Juno's temple in Rome alerted Marcus Manlius Capitolinus that the Gauls were invading in 390 BC. As all Roman Catholic priests are male, he is a **gander** – a male goose.

A family's Catholic leanings were often a relatively open secret and the authorities were more than likely to carry out spot checks and sudden raids on their homes (**Whither shall I wander?**). What they were looking for were the ingenious secret rooms, commonly called priest-holes, that many Catholics had built within their houses. These were as well hidden as possible – often concealed within a bedroom, possibly that of the lady of the house, with access confined to that particular room – since the queen's forces were notorious for looking everywhere (**Upstairs, downstairs/And in my lady's chamber**), pulling the house apart in the process.

If they found a priest-hole complete with a priest inside it, one test was to make him swear allegiance to the queen as head of the Church. This was something a true Catholic priest couldn't do (**There I met an old man/Who wouldn't say his prayers**). This refusal was tantamount to treason and left the authorities free to punish him as they saw fit (**I took him by the left leg/And threw him down the stairs**). The violence of the last line was just a precursor of the much nastier things (torture, hanging, drawing and quartering) that were inevitably to follow. To play 'Find the Priest' was the sixteenth-century children's version of today's bloodthirsty shoot-'em-up computer games – only this game was all too real (see ORANGES AND LEMONS).

# The Grand Old Duke of York

THE Grand old Duke of York,
He had ten thousand men.
He marched them up to the top of the hill
And he marched them down again.

And when they were up, they were up;
And when they were down, they were down.
And when they were only halfway up,
They were neither up nor down.

The Duke of York has historically been the title of the reigning monarch's second son, the Prince of Wales being that of the firstborn, and so the **Grand Old Duke of York** could have been any of them down the years. But investigation into English military history narrows down the search to just one candidate – Prince Frederick (1763–1827), son of 'mad' King George III and whose elder brother is the subject of another well-known rhyme (see GEORGIE PORGIE). Indeed, both brothers have starred in more than their fair share of rhymes.

One theory, popular in Yorkshire, relates to the purchase of Allerton Castle, a grade one listed Gothic mansion close to Harrogate, by Prince Frederick in 1786. This Duke of York had much of the place rebuilt before selling it soon afterwards in 1789. Part of his programme of renovation was the construction of what he called his Temple of

Victory – named after the Roman temple on the Palatine Hill in Rome – on the top of a 200-foot hill clearly visible for miles around. To this day, travellers can see the Temple as they drive along the A1 between Harrogate and York. Local legend has it that the worker-ant-like activity of the duke's **men** carrying materials up and down the hill inspired the famous rhyme.

A more convincing argument pinpointing Prince Frederick's claim to be the Grand Old Duke has been traced to the French Revolutionary Wars (1792–1802). In 1793, he was appointed field marshal and given a simple brief – invade France! Never a great military leader, however, Frederick failed to win the trust and confidence of his men and, despite a small victory over French forces at Beaumont in April 1794, he was trounced at Tourcoing in May and consequently relieved of his position. The hill he is supposed to have marched his men up and down before having them accidentally slaughtered is thought to be Mont Cassell, in northern France, standing nearly 600 feet above the Flanders coastal plain.

But that wasn't the end of the military career of the Grand Old Duke of York, as he was back in action five years later, in 1799, this time having been appointed commander-in-chief of the British forces by his less than sane father. In 1799, he was sent to join allied Russian forces to invade Holland. However, soon after the Duke of York arrived upon the scene, both discipline and morale among his men crumbled. The duke's lack of military experience as a field commander was apparent and, after he signed the Convention of Alkmaar on 10 October that year, a humiliating withdrawal was ordered.

Some researchers believe that 'The Grand Old Duke of York' was written to mock Frederick's hapless campaigns, in which many a hill would no doubt have been climbed, although he is now remembered in a more positive way – for his later wide-ranging reforms of the British forces that introduced the training and structural improvements that, in turn, paved the way for the military successes of Admiral Nelson and the Duke of Wellington. Under Frederick's overall command, these two military heroes eventually crushed Napoleon and his imperial fleet and army at Trafalgar (1805) and Waterloo (1815) respectively.

But there is another Duke of York who also fits the profile – James II, second son of King Charles I (see ROCK-A-BYE, BABY). This theory centres on the Glorious Revolution of

1688 when the king marched his army from London to Salisbury Plain to confront William of Orange, only to discover many of his closest allies, including the Duke of Marlborough, had switched allegiance and were now lined up on the side of the Dutch invader. This surprise discovery caused King James to beat a hasty retreat (**He marched them down again**), or so the story goes. The nursery rhyme neatly demotes the greatly disliked, openly Catholic king back to his former title, much as his own actions did.

I wonder what future nursery rhymes might be influenced by our own present royal family. Let's face it, the current Duke of York, Prince Andrew, might have been a bit of a lad when he was younger, but it is looking increasingly likely that the future Duke of York, Prince Harry, may eclipse all who went before. Here's to interesting times!

## Hark, Hark, the Dogs Do Bark

> HARK, hark, the dogs do bark,
> The beggars are coming to town;
> Some in rags
> And some in jags
> And one in a velvet gown.

This rhyme is generally thought to be about the destitution caused by the Dissolution of the Monasteries during the 1530s (see LITTLE JACK HORNER). The displacement of so many monks and nuns, and all the other folk who relied upon them either for a living or for charity, led to tens of thousands of homeless people wandering from town to town and city to city, in search of food and shelter. Between 1531 and 1598, laws were passed that laid down severe punishment for vagrants, including whipping, branding, enforced slavery and even execution for a second offence. The rhyme is thought to relate directly to these groups of people and their uninvited appearance in an otherwise peaceful hamlet or village. If this is the case, then the words are self-explanatory (**jags** being tatty items of clothing, or 'jagged' clothes, rather than luxury motor vehicles).

In 1572, Elizabeth I's government finally acknowledged that there were genuine cases of poverty and began to distinguish between the 'dishonest poor' and the 'impotent [i.e. powerless] poor'. Local magistrates were given the authority to start collecting a 'poor tax', which was used to provide workhouses, hospitals for the poor and doss houses. An effective piece of legislation, it was a forerunner of the modern welfare state that helped substantially to reduce poverty over the next two centuries until the Poor Law Act replaced it in 1834.

There is another theory about the origins of the rhyme that could have some basis in fact. During the seventeenth century, the English and the Dutch were generally at loggerheads over trade routes and control of the sea, as the four trade wars between 1652 and 1684, the Anglo-Dutch Wars, would suggest. So when the Dutch took over the English throne, this time in the person of William of Orange in the Glorious Revolution of 1688, some people were furious and they wanted everyone to know about it (**Hark, hark, the dogs do bark**).

The Beghards were a religious group originating in Europe, including the Netherlands, during the thirteenth and fourteenth centuries. Members lived a monastic lifestyle and were usually of humble origin or fallen on hard times. With such associations, it is easy to see how 'Beghard' would have become a derogatory term, the word 'beggar' stemming from it. Hence the English, who had long held the Dutch in great contempt, insulted them by likening their people to tramps and vagrants by calling them Beghards or **beggars**. It is therefore highly possible that the nursery rhyme evolved from a countrywide hue and cry as William of Orange, the man **in a velvet gown**, marched his band of Dutch 'Beghards' through the towns and villages to victory over James II.

# Hector Protector

HECTOR Protector was dressed all in green,
Hector Protector was sent to the queen;
The queen did not like him
And nor did the king,
So Hector Protector was sent back again.

At first glance, it would be fair to assume that the real **Hector Protector** would be one of the more famous Lord Protectors of England, the title given to the head of state

standing in for the monarch or replacing the monarch altogether, as during the latter years of the English Commonwealth (1649–60). The best-known Protector was Oliver
Cromwell (see HICKORY, DICKORY, DOCK), but he was
known for not liking the **queen** and the **king**, rather than
their not liking him.

There is another, far more likely, candidate in Richard
Plantagenet, Duke of York (1411–60). The fifteenth century
was a time of great turmoil in England. When Richard
arrived on the political scene, the Hundred Years' War
with France (1337–1453) was still being fought (with Joan
of Arc causing trouble all over the place), skirmishes with
the Scots, Welsh and Irish were breaking out along the
borders, and the Wars of the Roses (1455–87), between
the Yorkists and Lancastrians, were just around the corner
(see HEY DIDDLE DIDDLE), sparked off by events that
were about to unfold. The two central figures during this
time were King Henry VI (1421–71), of the House of
Lancaster, and his arch-rival, the Duke of York. For his
part in a plot against Henry V, Richard's father had been
stripped of his land and titles, and executed. When his
uncle, the previous Duke of York, who had remained loyal
to the Crown, died heroically on the battlefield of Agincourt a few months later in 1415, the young Richard was
permitted to inherit his titles and estates. When Henry V
was succeeded by his son, Henry VI, the duke and the new
king had a turbulent relationship right from the beginning.
In a clear snub, Richard was left out of the king's first
council, formed in 1439.

Over the years that followed, Richard staked out his own claim to the throne, via lineage from his great-grandfather, Edward III, and when that failed he declared his loyalty to the king in a bid to become his rightful heir. Unfortunately for Richard's plans, Henry VI was married to the formidable Margaret of Anjou. The queen had steered clear of affairs of state until the Duke of York started to pose an active threat to her husband, at which point she tried her utmost to block him at every turn (**The queen did not like him / And nor did the king**).

Then in 1453 King Henry suffered a complete mental breakdown, possibly brought on by the news of the defeat of his army at the Battle of Castillon. Richard seized his chance and insisted on forming a Great Council, after which the king's supporters were banished to the Tower of London. Despite strong opposition from Margaret of Anjou, the Duke of York was then appointed **Protector** of the Realm and Chief Councillor.

But, within two years and with the help of his queen, King Henry had made a full recovery, released his allies from the Tower, reversed most of Richard's actions and sent him back to Yorkshire (**So Hector Protector was sent back again**). Predictably, Richard then wasted little time in raising an army and succeeded in arresting Henry at the Battle of St Albans on 2 May 1455, although the king was soon released after agreeing to grant York and his supporters a major role in future affairs of state.

Then trouble flared up again, coming to a crunch at the Battle of Ludford Bridge in 1459, and Richard was again banished, this time to Ireland. With her husband once again held prisoner – captured by Richard's ally the Earl of Warwick at the Battle of Northampton in 1460, effectively rendering Richard and Warwick rulers of the country – the queen decided to take over and began to raise her own army in Wales and in the north of England. When her soldiers confronted the Duke of York – who had sneaked back from exile and proclaimed himself king – at the Battle of Wakefield (1460), they captured the duke, his son and his brother-in-law the Earl of Salisbury. All three were executed the following day and the former Protector's head was then displayed upon the gates of the city of York.

Despite his grisly demise, York must have had a genuine claim to the throne as his son Edward became king of England only a few months later, on 4 March 1461, after Henry VI had succumbed to another bout of madness. Queen Margaret fought bravely on until the Battle of Tewkesbury on 4 May 1471, where she was defeated and her son, her chosen heir to the throne, was killed. Margaret had gained a reputation as a ruthless and aggressive warrior but with the news of her husband's murder in the Tower of London on 21 May 1471 and with her son dead, her spirit was crushed and she languished in captivity until she was ransomed by the French king. Only then did she finally return to Anjou, in France, dying in 1482.

And that is the story of the real Hector the Protector, although these days he is better known in his guise of a cartoon dolphin designed to teach children how to use the internet safely.

# Here We Go Round the Mulberry Bush

HERE we go round the mulberry bush,
The mulberry bush, the mulberry bush;
Here we go round the mulberry bush,
On a cold and frosty morning.

This is the way we wash our clothes,
Wash our clothes, wash our clothes;
This is the way we wash our clothes,
On a cold and frosty morning.

This is the way we iron our clothes,
Iron our clothes, iron our clothes;
This is the way we iron our clothes,
On a cold and frosty morning.

This is the way we scrub the floor,
Scrub the floor, scrub the floor;
This is the way we scrub the floor,
On a cold and frosty morning.

This is the way we mend our clothes,
Mend our clothes, mend our clothes;
This is the way we mend our clothes,
On a cold and frosty morning.

This is the way we sweep the house,
Sweep the house, sweep the house;
This is the way we sweep the house,
On a cold and frosty morning.

This is the way we bake our bread,
Bake our bread, bake our bread;
This is the way we bake our bread,
On a cold and frosty morning.

This is the way we go to church,
Go to church, go to church;
This is the way we go to church,
On a cold and frosty morning.

Here we go round the mulberry bush,
The mulberry bush, the mulberry bush;
Here we go round the mulberry bush,
On a cold and frosty morning.

The **mulberry bush** has had its place in legend for hundreds of years, most famously in the tragic story of Pyramus and Thisbe, a version of which is told by the Latin author Gaius Julius Hyginus (*c*.64 BC–AD 17), and, centuries later, camped up in comic fashion by Bottom and companions in William Shakespeare's *A Midsummer Night's Dream*. The tale is set in ancient Babylon, where two children, Pyramus and Thisbe, grew up as next-door neighbours. As the years passed and they became young adults, the pair fell in love, but their parents forbade them to see each other. Instead, the lovers communicated secretly through a hole in the wall that separated their two houses. One night they decided to run away together and marry in secret.

Pyramus described to Thisbe a location marked by a mulberry bush. She arrived at the rendezvous first but, while she was waiting for Pyramus, she was scared by a passing lion, its jaws still bloodied from a recent kill. In panic, Thisbe dropped her cloak and ran to hide in a nearby cave. When Pyramus arrived, he found his lover's blood-stained cloak on the floor and fresh lion tracks all round. He had always been hot-headed and, overcome with grief that his sweetheart appeared to have been eaten by a lion, he unsheathed his sword and stabbed himself in the heart. Meanwhile Thisbe had been waiting to make sure the lion really had gone, and as soon as she thought it was safe, she returned to the mulberry bush, only to discover what her lover, the fool, had done. Every bit as impulsive as her beloved, she tugged the sword out of Pyramus's heart and plunged it into her own, spraying blood – both hers and his – all over the white mulberries. In tribute to the lovers, the mulberries remained red, instead of white, and have stayed this colour ever since. The moral of this story clearly is: don't kill yourself for love. (Not that lovers ever heed such advice, as the star-crossed Romeo and Juliet – in another of Shakespeare's plays, with a very similar ending to this ancient tale – make quite plain.)

'Here We Go Round the Mulberry Bush' is one of the many 'repetitive' nursery rhymes that can easily be adapted and added to, and probably has been many times over the years, to suit any occasion. There are similar versions in Holland and Scandinavia, although a juniper bush is understandably substituted for a mulberry bush in those rather colder countries. This song could be extended to last all day if necessary. Essentially, it's a worker's song devised to pass away the time and improve morale. For example, working miners might sing 'This is the way we dig for coal, dig for coal, etc.' and a version for soldiers might go 'This is the way we march to war'. Sailors might sing 'This is the way we mend our sails, mend our sails' while school children might chant 'This is the way we brush our teeth', and so on.

For the origins of this nursery rhyme, we need to travel to the unlikely setting of HMP Wakefield and the exercise yard. According to R. S. Duncan, a former governor of Wakefield and author of a fascinating history of the prisons that have existed on the same site for over five hundred years, the mulberry tree in the exercise yard provides the root (or roots) of this long-standing rhyme. Mulberry trees have been associated with prisons since the early nineteenth century, when many prison governors entered the profitable British silk industry, mulberry leaves being the preferred food of silkworms.

Duncan insists that, back in the days when Wakefield was a House of Correction, female prisoners used to walk their children around the mulberry tree planted in the courtyard and devised the rhyme to help pass the time and keep the children occupied. According to the Wakefield tourist office, a mulberry tree thrives to this day within the prison grounds.

With the possibility of the rhyme being written in prison, its meaning changes to something much darker. After all, it's not summer but **a cold and frosty morning**. The activities listed in the song are no longer simple chores but the catalogue of wearisome tasks performed by a female prisoner in a House of Correction: washing, ironing and mending clothes, scrubbing the floor, sweeping and baking bread, all topped off with a compulsory visit to church. The repetition within the verse (**This is the way we scrub the floor, / Scrub the floor, scrub the floor**) emphasizes the dreary endlessness of the tasks – ones that have to be done a certain way. More than just a worker's song, 'Here We Go Round the Mulberry Bush' would seem to be the nursery-rhyme equivalent of a song chanted by a chain gang (see SWING LOW, SWEET CHARIOT).

# Hey Diddle Diddle

HEY diddle diddle,
The cat and the fiddle,
The cow jumped over the moon;
The little dog laughed to see such fun,
And the dish ran away with the spoon.

Often described as one of the best-known nonsense poems of all time, there have been some interesting and diverse attempts to explain what inspired it. Here are a few of my favourites.

The first example is a story that explains Richard III's path to the English throne. On 9 April 1483, Richard's brother King Edward IV died, leaving the throne to his thirteen-year-old son, Edward V. Richard then governed as regent for the young king and placed Edward and his younger brother in the Tower of London, supposedly for their own safety. However, within weeks both boys had been declared illegitimate by an Act of Parliament, known as 'Titulus Regius' (or 'Royal Title' in Latin), after which the 'Princes in the Tower' mysteriously disappeared. Richard was then declared king of England on 6 July 1483. Many people were deeply sceptical about what had gone on, but it was far too dangerous to openly question the new king's actions. It was time to invent a new nursery rhyme and one that started with a nonsensical opening line (**Hey diddle diddle**) to throw the suspicious off the scent.

### The cat and the fiddle

Sir William Catesby (1450–85) was a leading member of the powerful group of men who supported Richard's claim to the throne. After Richard had been declared king, he quickly rose to power, first as Chancellor of the Exchequer and then Speaker of the House during the Parliament of 1484. Catesby was one of the few who had Richard III's full support and confidence, and was known publicly as the **'Catte'**.

*The cow jumped over the moon*

Richard Neville (1428–71) was the 16th Earl of Warwick and 6th Earl of Salisbury. A powerful and influential person in royal circles, he became known as the 'Kingmaker'.

He was a leading figure during the Wars of the Roses (1455–87) and responsible for deposing the Lancastrian

monarch, Henry VI (see HECTOR PROTECTOR), replacing
him with the Yorkist king Edward IV, Richard III's elder
brother. Warwick was also Richard's cousin, the future
king having spent much of his formative years in his care at
Warwick Castle, eventually marrying Anne Neville, the Earl
of Warwick's youngest daughter. The Warwick family
emblem at the time was said to have been a **cow**.

Neville's cousin was Henry Percy, 2nd Earl of Northum-
berland (1392–1455), but when the two families found
themselves on opposing sides during the Wars of the Roses,
a long-running and bitter feud developed. The Nevilles
eventually prevailed, with the accession of kings Edward
and Richard. The Percy family emblem was said to be a
moon. Hence: **The cow jumped over the moon.**

*The little dog laughed to see such fun*

Francis Lovell (Viscount Lovell, 1454–87) was the king's
childhood friend. The pair fought together to suppress the
Buckingham Rebellion in 1483 and Lovell's influence was
well known throughout England. His family emblem was a
**dog**. (Another popular rhyme of the day shows how cus-
tomary it was to refer to the powerful by their symbols:
'The Catte, the Ratte and Lovell our Dog rule all England
under a hog'.) Obviously, the 'dog' was more than satisfied
to hear of his friend's rise to power as he was immediately
knighted and given a castle (**The little dog laughed to see
such fun**).

### And the dish ran away with the spoon

This is where the story starts sounding rather thin. The argument goes that Richard himself was the **dish** while the **spoon** was either the anointing spoon used during the coronation or the royal sceptre that he had run away with – although it is hard to find a reference in this vein to Richard III. Perhaps we should stick with Shakespeare, who draws our attention to the dish of revenge (best served cold) in his play about these events, *Richard III*. This interpretation of the rhyme makes a good tale, although, sadly, there is little evidence that the Neville or Percy family emblems ever included either a cow or the moon.

Theory two travels two hundred years on to Queen Elizabeth I (1533–1603), who was well known for giving members of her court nicknames. Apparently the Virgin Queen herself is the **cat** and other characters among her entourage were known as the **moon**, the **cow** and the lapdog. The **spoon** was thought to be the royal food taster and the **dish** was the queen's serving girl. When the two of them eloped (**the dish ran away with the spoon**), the jealous queen was enraged and had them hunted down and thrown into the Tower of London.

Theory three, and my favourite, is the idea that the entire riddle is in fact a lesson in stargazing. There are certain nights of the year, usually in April, where particular constellations all appear close to the moon at the same time. The line-up is the **Cat** (Leo), the **Cow** (Taurus), the **Little**

**Dog** (Canis Minor), the **Dish** (Crater, a dish-shaped constellation), the **Spoon** (Ursa Major – Big Dipper in the US, or the Plough in Britain), the **Fiddle** (Lyra) and the **moon** (that will be the moon, then). The theory goes that the rhyme was developed as a way to remind children of the planting season in early spring. In other words, when all of the constellations line up close to the moon in the night sky, then it is time for farmers and smallholders to sow their seeds.

## Hickory, Dickory, Dock

> HICKORY, dickory, dock,
> The mouse ran up the clock.
> The clock struck one,
> The mouse ran down,
> Hickory, dickory, dock.

This rhyme, first published in 1743, is believed by some to have been inspired by the last man ever to rule England as a republic.

After the execution of Charles I in 1649, England became a commonwealth for eleven years (1649–60), during which time a protectorate was established (1653–9), with Oliver Cromwell holding the title of Lord Protector of the Commonwealth of England, Scotland and Ireland. Just prior to his death, on 3 September 1658, the arch-republican head of state surprised many by nominating his eldest surviving son, Richard, to succeed him.

Richard Cromwell was born on 4 October 1626 and is believed to have served as a captain in Sir Thomas Fairfax's

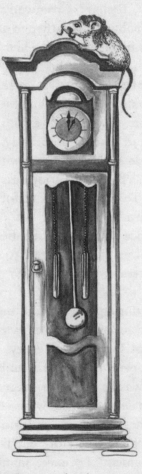

New Model Army during the late 1640s, although with apparently little distinction as nothing is known of his

service. In 1649, he married Dorothy, the daughter of Richard Maijor, and settled on the family estate at Hursley. During the 1650s, Richard Cromwell's lack of ambition appeared to be troubling his father to the point where, in 1653, he was not included in the elder Cromwell's 'Bare-bones Parliament', although his younger brother Henry was. When Oliver became Lord Protector in 1653, Richard was offered no public role and instead his father wrote to Richard Maijor: 'I would have him mind and understand business, read history and study cosmography and mathematics – these things are good, with subordination to the things of God. Better than idleness or mere outward worldly contents. There are things fit for public service, for which a man is born.'

But, in accordance with the constitution of the Protectorate, Oliver Cromwell was required to name, or at least nominate, a successor, and in 1657 began to include Richard in affairs of state. In June of that year, he was at his father's side during his second installation as Lord Protector, and the following month was given the role of Lord Chancellor at Oxford University. By December, the prodigal son had even become a member of the Council of State. But he wasn't ready to succeed his father after Oliver Cromwell's death the following year.

Unlike his father, Richard had no real military or political experience and therefore cut little ice with either the army or Parliament. To make matters worse, he had inherited a regime that was in debt to the tune of £2 million – billions in today's terms – and measures had to be taken.

In April 1659, when Parliament threatened cuts to reduce army funding, the generals presented a petition to Richard Cromwell which he passed on to Parliament. Ignoring the petition, Parliament instead passed two resolutions banning any meetings of army officers without the express permission of the Lord Protector and Parliament, and demanding that officers swear an oath that they would never disrupt or prevent the business of Parliament by force. The army responded by demanding the dissolution of Parliament. Richard refused and hostile troops began to gather at St James's in London. Having given in to the troops' demands, his next mistake was to refuse an offer of heavily armed support from the French ambassador. By now, he was being ridiculed and mocked by enemies and supporters alike, his nicknames ranging from Queen Dick to Tumbledown Dick and Hickory Dick. Before the year was out, Richard had effectively been forced out of office and the monarchy restored in the shape of King Charles II.

And this leads neatly to the suggestion that 'Hickory, Dickory, Dock' is directly connected with the ineffectual Richard Cromwell (**Hickory Dick**) and his one-year reign (**The clock struck one, / The mouse ran down**). The second (rarely used) verse would also appear to be about Richard's rapid rise from nowhere (**The pig flew up in the air**) and back down again, ousted from the throne by Charles II (**The man in brown / Soon brought him down**):

Dickory, dickory, dare,
The pig flew up in the air.
The man in brown
Soon brought him down,
Dickory, dickory, dare.

# Higgledy, Piggledy, My Black Hen

HIGGLEDY, piggledy, my black hen,
She lays eggs for gentlemen,
Sometimes nine and sometimes ten;
Gentlemen come every day
To see what my black hen has laid.

The clue as to how to read this rhyme is in the opening words. Indicating a state of confusion and disorder, the expression **higgledy, piggledy** was first recorded at the end of the fifteenth century. There are various other versions of the phrase, such as 'higly pigly', but the key thing is that they all appear to involve pigs, or the confused herding together of these animals. Pigs have long been conventionally considered the dirtiest animals in the farmyard, living in a state of squalor – if you're ever tempted to refer to a teenager's bedroom as a pigsty, you're using the same idea. But it's no farmyard that's being described in this rhyme; it's a house of ill-repute, a brothel. The narrator is a pimp or procurer, **my black hen** is a prostitute and the **gentlemen** are her clients.

A similar rhyme, dating from the eighteenth century, makes a much clearer allusion to the subject:

> Little Blue Betty lived in a den,
> She sold good ale to gentlemen;
> Gentlemen came every day
> And little Blue Betty hopped away;
> She hopped upstairs to make her bed
> And tumbled down and broke her head.

# Hot Cross Buns

> HOT cross buns, hot cross buns!
> One a penny two a penny, hot cross buns!
> If you have no daughters, give them to your sons.
> One a penny two a penny, hot cross buns!

Two festive foods both connected with Easter – pancakes on Shrove Tuesday and hot cross buns on Good Friday – have survived into the present even though most traditional aspects of their special days have long ceased to have any widespread resonance. There was once, however, a superstition that good luck would accompany those who ate them and bad luck those who did not. Hence this song – traditionally sung by hawkers and street traders, eager, in any case, to sell their wares – appears to remind potential purchasers that they should make sure everyone they knew ate the buns (**If you have no daughters, give them to your**

**sons**). A further couple of lines, sometimes added, offer further encouragement:

> But if you haven't any of these pretty little elves
> You cannot do better than eat them yourselves.

In more recent times, the poor old hot cross bun has come under pressure from a variety of directions. In 2003, for instance, four local councils decided to ban them for fear of offending non-Christians. The bun has also attracted speculation about its ancient pagan origins despite its bearing the overtly Christian symbol of a cross and being sold on the day of the Crucifixion, and this has, paradoxically, prompted some devout Christians to refuse to eat them. The wildest piece of evidence cited to support this is based on the similarity of the word 'bun' to the ancient Greek word *boun* which, according to the eighteenth-century antiquary Jacob Bryant, was a cake with two horns, offered to the gods at Arkite temples every seventh day.

More credible is the association of the buns with an ancient British festival. Easter is believed to derive from the Anglo-Saxon festival of Eostre – a pagan goddess, possibly of the dawn, her name deriving from the same word that gives us 'east' – celebrated at the spring equinox. According to this interpretation, the cross on the bun symbolizes the four quarters of the moon. Whether or not this particular marking has pre-Christian origins, it is known that cakes were often baked in honour of the gods.

# The House That Jack Built

THIS is the house that Jack built.

This is the malt
That lay in the house that Jack built.

This is the rat that ate the malt
That lay in the house that Jack built.

This is the cat that killed the rat
That ate the malt
That lay in the house that Jack built.

This is the dog that worried the cat
That killed the rat that ate the malt
That lay in the house that Jack built.

This is the cow with the crumpled horn
That tossed the dog that worried the cat
That killed the rat that ate the malt
That lay in the house that Jack built.

This is the maiden all forlorn
That milked the cow with the crumpled horn
That tossed the dog that worried the cat
That killed the rat that ate the malt
That lay in the house that Jack built.

This is the man all tattered and torn
That kissed the maiden all forlorn
That milked the cow with the crumpled horn
That tossed the dog that worried the cat
That killed the rat that ate the malt
That lay in the house that Jack built.

This is the priest all shaven and shorn
That married the man all tattered and torn
That kissed the maiden all forlorn
That milked the cow with the crumpled horn
That tossed the dog that worried the cat
That killed the rat that ate the malt
That lay in the house that Jack built.

This is the cock that crowed in the morn
That waked the priest all shaven and shorn
That married the man all tattered and torn
That kissed the maiden all forlorn
That milked the cow with the crumpled horn
That tossed the dog that worried the cat
That killed the rat that ate the malt
That lay in the house that Jack built.

This is the farmer sowing his corn
That kept the cock that crowed in the morn
That waked the priest all shaven and shorn
That married the man all tattered and torn
That kissed the maiden all forlorn
That milked the cow with the crumpled horn
That tossed the dog that worried the cat
That killed the rat that ate the malt
That lay in the house that Jack built.

'The House That Jack Built' first appeared in 1755, in
*Nurse Truelove's New Year's Gift, or The Book of Books
for Children*, its relentlessly cumulative verses inspired by

a Hebrew hymn in the Jewish book of rituals *Sepher Haggadah*.

This rhyme has been used ever since as a memory-improving device but also to remind children that everything has a consequence. Each part of the ever-expanding list is dependent on the last, just as in FOR WANT OF A NAIL. The series of events also builds up a picture of English country life during the eighteenth century – clearly quite action-packed in Jack's neck of the woods. To this day, the rhyme's refrain is used as a derogatory term for any badly designed or built property, the phrase **the house that Jack built** – Jack generally being a lazy fellow in English folklore – evoking an image of something that is about to fall down.

# Humpty Dumpty

HUMPTY Dumpty sat on the wall,
Humpty Dumpty had a great fall;
All the king's horses and all the king's men
Couldn't put Humpty together again.

The real Humpty Dumpty was a powerful cannon used by the Royalist forces during the English Civil War of 1642 to 1651. Sir Charles Lucas and Sir George Lisle led the king's men and overpowered the Parliament stronghold of Colchester early in 1648. They grimly held on to it while the Parliamentarians, led by Thomas Fairfax, encircled and

besieged the town in what became known as the Siege of
Colchester. The supporters of Charles I almost won the day
– all thanks to his doughtiest defender, **Humpty Dumpty**.

In pole position, as it were, on top of the church tower of
St Mary-at-the-Walls, One-Eyed Thompson, the gunner,
managed to blast away the attacking Roundhead troops
with rousing success for eleven whole weeks. That is, until
the top of the church tower was eventually blown away,
sending Humpty Dumpty crashing to the ground outside

the city wall, where it buried itself in deep marshland. The king's cavalry (the **horses**) and the infantry (the **men**) hurried to retrieve the cannon in order to repair it, but they **couldn't put Humpty together again** and without their weapon of mass destruction they were soon overrun by Fairfax and his soldiers.

There are another two verses preceding the better-known one that tell the tale in more detail:

> In sixteen hundred and forty-eight,
> When England suffered the pains of state,
> The Roundheads laid siege to Colchester town
> Where the king's men still fought for the crown.
>
> There One-Eyed Thompson stood on the wall,
> A gunner of deadliest aim of all.
> From St Mary's Tower his cannon he fired,
> Humpty Dumpty was its name.

Written in the same vein as 'Hitler has only Got One Ball' (a song mocking the Nazis that raised the British spirits during the darker days of the Second World War), 'Humpty Dumpty' was a piece of propaganda that passed from town to town as the news of the king's defeat spread across England and the Parliamentarian troops slowly returned home, teaching even their youngest children to recite the tale of their victory.

But if the rhyme is entirely military in origin, how come we all think of Humpty Dumpty as an egg? The answer to that question is found in the late nineteenth century in

Lewis Carroll's *Through the Looking-Glass* (1871). Sir John Tenniel's iconic illustration shows Alice in deep discussion with Humpty Dumpty as he sits upon a high wall. Tenniel, clearly taken with the idea of the impossibility of Humpty Dumpty's being put back together again once he'd fallen off the wall, has him shaped as an egg with short arms and legs. This is the first known depiction of Humpty as an egg, one that was to become the definitive image. (For other rhymes illustrated by Tenniel, see THE QUEEN OF HEARTS and TWEEDLEDUM AND TWEEDLEDEE.)

# I Had a Little Nut Tree

I had a little nut tree,
Nothing would it bear
But a silver nutmeg
And a golden pear.

The King of Spain's daughter
Came to visit me,
And all for the sake
Of my little nut tree.

Her dress was made of crimson,
Jet black was her hair,
She asked me for my nut tree
And my golden pear.

> I said, 'So fair a princess
> Never did I see;
> I will give you all the fruit
> From my little nut tree.'

In 1501, the Spanish king Ferdinand and his queen Isabella I agreed that their beautiful youngest daughter, Catherine of Aragon, should become the bride of Henry VII's fifteen-year-old son and heir, Arthur.

Arthur and Catherine's marriage bonded the royal families of England and Spain. But it was short-lived because the young prince died of fever the following year. Faced with the prospect of returning her dowry to Spain, Henry immediately arranged a new marriage for Catherine, this time with his second son and new heir, also called Henry. As he was five years younger than Catherine, however, the Spanish princess had to wait, isolated from court, until her new fiancé was old enough to marry.

It is thought that the nursery rhyme sums up the royal manoeuvrings of the time. The **nut tree** is England itself. The king is offering its 'fruits' (English wealth) to the King of Spain's daughter. The objects in question and the precious metals they are made of hint at why both countries were so keen to agree to a second marriage. Together the two nations could consolidate their success in trade – with spices from the East (symbolized by the **nutmeg**) and precious metals from South America (**silver ... golden**) – thereby substantially increasing the wealth of both countries. The **pear** is perhaps a reference to England's own agricultural plenty, from which Spain might also benefit.

Catherine was to become a popular princess and, later, a much loved queen. Unfortunately her marriage to Henry VIII ended much less happily than it had started. When, after many years, she had been unable to bear the king a son, and therefore a legitimate heir, she was cast aside in favour of Anne Boleyn (see THREE BLIND MICE). The English people never forgave Anne for ruining what they regarded as the king's rightful marriage and Henry's second queen was known for the rest of her short life as the Great Whore.

## In Marble Walls as White as Milk

> IN marble walls as white as milk,
> Lined with a skin as smooth as silk,
> Within a fountain colour clear,
> A golden sphere doth there appear;
> No doors are found in this stronghold,
> Yet thieves break in and steal the gold.

First published in John Newbery's *Mother Goose's Melody* in 1765, this rhyme is actually a riddle that the reader is expected to solve. A riddle is an ambiguous statement, or puzzle, that can have several answers, although only one can be correct, and riddles have been popular since ancient times. As long ago as 400 BC, Plato is known to have observed children learning riddles; they feature in Old

Norse literature and in Old English poetry, most notably in the Exeter Book – a collection of manuscripts originally housed in Exeter Cathedral – dating from around AD 800. While mostly frivolous, riddles can be profound, and even life-threatening: in perhaps the most celebrated riddle-posing session of all time, Oedipus has to give the correct answer to the Sphinx in order to avoid being killed. While the rhyme above is hardly in this category, in keeping with time-honoured tradition, I'm not going to give you the answer, but I will give you a clue. It's not the Bank of England, although you might go to work on it. (For other riddling rhymes, see As I Was Going to St Ives and Flour of England.)

## Jack and Jill

JACK and Jill went up the hill
To fetch a pail of water;
Jack fell down and broke his crown,
And Jill came tumbling after.

Up Jack got and down he trot,
As fast as he could caper;
He went to bed and covered his head
With vinegar and brown paper.

This has been traditionally seen as pure nonsense verse, and indeed, taken at face value, the rhyme doesn't make sense.

Why do Jack and Jill go *up* the hill to fetch water? We don't see many wells or springs on top of a hill, do we? Water generally runs downhill, hence the bottom of a hill or a valley is the best place to look for it. There must be more to this rhyme than first meets the eye.

One popular suggestion for its origin is that Louis XVI of France and his queen, the infamous Marie Antoinette, are Jack and Jill. But the only real supporting evidence for that

is the idea that Jack **broke** (or lost) **his crown** and that **Jill came tumbling after** him, or at least her head did. The executions of the French royal family took place in 1793, and the poem was first published in 1795, so this interpretation does at first seem plausible.

Closer to home (and probably to reality), a small village in Somerset has laid claim to the origin of the rhyme. The story told in Kilmersdon is that during 1697 the village was home to a young unmarried couple who did a lot of their courting up on a hill, away from the prying eyes of the local gossips. Consequently Jill became pregnant, but just before the baby was born Jack was killed by a rock that fell off the hill and landed on his head. Only days later, Jill also died in childbirth. It's cheery stuff. The nursery rhyme is these days depicted on a series of tablet stones along the path to the hill, the people of Kilmersdon being convinced of their association with the famous nursery rhyme.

For the third theory, we must travel back a further fifty years in history, and from love to alcohol. Some researchers believe King Charles I (1600–49), who, during his reign, attempted to reform taxes on alcohol, provided the real inspiration for the rhyme. It is claimed that he was prevented from raising taxes by Parliament on several occasions and so, instead, he reduced the actual measures alcohol could be served in. Up until that point, wines and ales could be bought as a pint, a half pint, known as a 'Jack', or a quarter pint, known as a 'Gill' (pronounced in the same way as the 'gill' of a fish) – hence **Jill**. As the measures **came tumbling** down, Charles had effectively gained his tax increase, as slightly less alcohol could then be bought for the same price. To this day, many beer glass manufacturers still mark a half-pint line on a pint glass with a crown to honour the day the Jack was decreased in volume by King Charles I. No wonder they cut his head off.

But in fact, Jack and Jill were written about even earlier, in 1595 to be precise, by William Shakespeare in *A Midsummer Night's Dream*: 'Jack shall have Jill; / Nought shall go ill.' It sounds as if Jack and Jill may well have been used in the past as a generic name for a couple, just as we'd say Janet and John today. But, this couple go even further back in history, it would appear, research taking us to twelfth-century Iceland.

Snorri Sturluson (1178–1241) was a politician, poet and noted historian. He was also the author of a collection of Old Norse poems, myths and tales. His *Gylfaginning* manuscript ('The Fooling of Gylfi') tells the famous ancient Norse tale of a young brother and sister, Hjuki (pronounced Juk-ee) and Bil, whom the moon god captured on a dark night as they stole a pail of water from the Bygrir Well. They were immediately spirited away to the moon, where they can be seen to this day carrying a bucket of water attached to a long pole. For nearly a thousand years, Scandinavians explained the markings of the lunar surface thus, just as we in England spoke to our own children about the man in the moon or how it was made of cheese. This tale is thought by many to be the original version of 'Jack and Jill' (see also THE MAN IN THE MOON).

# Jack, Be Nimble

JACK, be nimble,
Jack, be quick,
Jack, jump over
The candlestick.

'Jack, Be Nimble' was first published in 1798 and has re-appeared in various forms ever since. A couple of versions extend into a second verse:

Jack jumped high,
Jack jumped low,
Jack jumped over and burned his toe.

Over the years, children have used it as a skipping rhyme, no doubt with little thought about the origins of the poem, of which there are three very different theories.

One theory is based on the folk belief that yellow fever, or 'yellow Jack fever' – an acute viral disease that was rife in the West until vaccination was developed in the early twentieth century – could be prevented by the presence of fire. The most obvious symptom of fever is the body's rapid increase of temperature. By having another source of heat nearby, the fever could be drawn out, or so it was believed. During outbreaks, children were often put to bed with a burning candle beside their cots to ward off the illness.

Another suggestion runs that Jack was actually the notor-ious pirate captain Calico Jack Rackham (1682–1720), so

named because of his colourful calico clothing, and that
the rhyme celebrates his regular near-miss escapes from the
long arm of the law. Jack wasn't quite **nimble** enough, it

would appear, as he was eventually captured and hanged,
although the equally notorious Mary Read and Anne
Bonnie, members of his crew, were saved from execution

because of the 'innocent' unborn babies they were supposedly carrying.

There is no real evidence to back up either of these suggestions, however. The true origin of the rhyme goes back many centuries. Candle jumping in those times was a traditional method of predicting the future. Quite simply, if the candle stayed alight after a person had 'jumped it', then he or she could look forward to a bright and prosperous future. If, however, the flame went out, then things looked rather bleak. Although not as bleak, I imagine, as it would if the candle set light to the jumper's clothing as he/she passed over it, in which case his/her future would be short and phosphorous.

Candle jumping might be incorporated into other festivities, such as the feast of St Catherine on 25 November, when winter was drawing in and the days getting shorter and darker. Towards the end of the day, bonfires would be lit and fireworks set off, including, quite possibly, Catherine wheels – picturesquely named after the manner of the saint's martyrdom. Catherine is the patron saint of unmarried women and her festival gave spinsters the opportunity to openly search for a husband. During the festivities, men in costume danced and sang while the ladies served punch and showed off their buns. The whole mad event would be concluded with the placing of a tall candlestick on the ground over which people jumped, one after the other, while the crowd chanted the name of each jumper.

The game of candle leaping has a very long history, in fact, being related to fire leaping, which can be traced back to between five and ten thousand years ago. Bonfires – originally containing animal bones, which accounts for the name – were believed to ward off evil and dangerous spirits; hence many considered that jumping over the flames would bring good fortune – or a good husband.

## Jack Sprat

> JACK Sprat could eat no fat,
> His wife could eat no lean,
> And so between them both
> They licked the platter clean.

In 1190, King Richard I (the Lionheart) set off on the Third Crusade. Unfortunately, that left room for his younger brother John to try and take control. It was a turbulent time for England. The youngest of the four princes (Jack Sprat), John was a highly unpopular figure – nicknamed John Lackland for his lack of territories and John Softsword for his lack of military success. The attempt by John and his greedy wife, Isabella of Gloucester, to claim the throne was regarded as an act of treachery, although Richard later forgave his younger sibling.

John is now best known as the enemy of the fictional hero Robin Hood. While the ballads were inspired by his apparent greed, it seems that the money wasn't for him, or not all of it, in any case. When Richard was captured and held hostage by Duke Leopold, 150,000 marks was demanded – a king's ransom in more ways than one. John and Isabella raised the funds by allegedly clearing out the coffers of England after finding they were unable to raise enough money from the royal vaults alone (**between them both / They licked the platter clean**). When Richard died in 1199, John took over as king but he was not an effective monarch and, tired of having their country mismanaged by a series of unreliable kings and queens, the barons famously forced him at Runnymede to sign the Magna Carta (1215), which limited the powers of the monarch and paved the way for modern democracy. In the words of Winston Churchill: 'When the long tally is added, it will be seen that the British nation and the English-speaking world owe far more to the vices of John than to the labours of virtuous sovereigns.'

In more recent times, one Jack Spratt appears as the main character in two novels, *The Big Over Easy* (2005) and *The Fourth Bear* (2006), by Jasper Fforde. This Jack, a detective inspector in the Reading police force, investigates the crimes committed by other nursery rhyme characters. Like his namesake in the rhyme, the detective inspector neatly trims all the fat from his food before he eats it because he claims his wife died from eating too much fat.

# Ladybird, Ladybird

LADYBIRD, ladybird, fly away home,
Your house is on fire and your children are gone;
All except one who is called little Ann,
For she crept under the frying pan.

'Ladybird, Ladybird' is, on the face of it, a gentle rhyme to sing to a black-and-red-spotted beetle if one happens to land upon your hand – always considered lucky. But if you read it carefully, it becomes more sinister. Why would anyone want to tell the ladybird her family is being destroyed in a fire, especially when it is most unlikely to be true?

For centuries, farmers and gardeners alike have actively encouraged ladybirds, as they eat aphids that might otherwise damage plants and crops. Hence one interpretation of the rhyme is that it is to encourage ladybirds to leave their land at the end of the season before the stubble is set on fire to make the fields ready for the next crop. But it appears that there's more to the rhyme than that . . .

The word **ladybird** in fact derives from the Catholic term for the Virgin Mary, 'Our Lady'. Hence some historians believe the rhyme offered a warning to Catholics who refused to attend Protestant services following enforcement of the Acts of Uniformity (1549–59). Instead, many would hold Mass in non-church settings, often outdoors in the

countryside or in a barn. Inevitably, such defiance was met with violence and many Catholic priests were burned at the stake for continuing to practise their faith so openly (see GOOSIE, GOOSIE GANDER).

# The Lion and the Unicorn

THE lion and the unicorn were fighting for the crown,
The lion beat the unicorn all around the town;
Some gave them white bread and some gave them brown,
Some gave them plum cake and drummed them out of town.

The origins of this nursery rhyme are rooted in the traditionally tense relationship between England and Scotland.
England, whose standard bore the emblem of a **lion,** and
Scotland, represented by a **unicorn,** had been at constant
odds with each other since long before the English invasion
of 1296. But this all calmed down when James VI of Scotland became James I of England in 1603, uniting the two
kingdoms under the Scottish Stuart dynasty. To this day,
the royal Coat of Arms for the United Kingdom bears both
the lion of England and the unicorn of Scotland.

Unfortunately, the Stuart monarchy didn't prove a particularly steady one and did not last long on the English
throne, as several of the other nursery rhymes show (see
REMEMBER, REMEMBER THE FIFTH OF NOVEMBER and
ROCK-A-BYE, BABY in particular). Not one but two Stuart
kings were sacked by Parliament and the people, and in
1714 the Hanoverian royal family took over.

Although technically now British citizens, the Scots had
remained loyal to the Stuart line, and when Charles Edward
Stuart, better known as Bonnie Prince Charlie, landed in
Scotland in 1745, many rallied to his cause and the Lion

and the Unicorn really were **fighting for the crown**. At first,
the Unicorn seemed to be winning, with victories at
Prestonpans and Carlisle. By the time they reached Derby,
his advisers forced Bonnie Prince Charlie to agree to retreat
to Scotland, as none of the English support he had been

promised had turned up and the Scots found themselves
far too exposed. But by now, George II's son, the Duke
of Cumberland, was hot on their heels and he caught up
with them at Culloden. Ignoring the advice of his best
commander, Lord George Murray, Charles chose to fight
on flat, open, marshy ground where his forces were exposed
to superior British firepower. But Charles was commanding
his army from a position from which he could not see what
was happening. Hoping that Cumberland's army would
attack first, he left his men exposed to Hanoverian artillery
for twenty minutes before finally ordering an attack. The

ill-thought-out battle was a disaster for the Jacobites: **The lion beat the unicorn all around the town.**

With that, the Jacobites were on the run and heavily dependent on the charity and cover of their remaining supporters, who helped as much as they could afford to: **Some gave them white bread and some gave them brown, / Some gave them plum cake.** But this was very dangerous for them to do as the Duke of Cumberland's troops committed so many atrocities in their relentless search for the fleeing rebels, that he was later nicknamed 'the Butcher' in Scotland. (See also ELSIE MARLEY.)

The most loyal supporters went to desperate measures to get their prince **out of town** – that is, Scotland – both for his sake and for their own. Bonnie Prince Charlie's subsequent flight has become the stuff of legend, and is commemorated in the THE SKYE BOAT SONG. Assisted by loyal supporters, he evaded capture and left the country aboard a French frigate called, ironically enough, *L'Heureux* – 'The Fortunate One'. In the end, the Lion had won.

# Little Bo Peep

LITTLE Bo Peep has lost her sheep
And doesn't know where to find them;
Leave them alone and they'll come home,
Bringing their tails behind them.

Little Bo Peep fell fast asleep
And dreamt she heard them bleating;
But when she awoke, she found it a joke,
For they were all still fleeting.

Then up she took her little crook,
Determined for to find them;
She found them indeed, but it made her heart bleed
For they'd left their tails behind them.

It happened one day, as Bo Peep did stray
Into a meadow hard by,
There she espied their tails side by side,
All hung on a tree to dry.

She heaved a sigh, and wiped her eye
And over the hillocks went rambling,
And tried what she could, as a shepherdess should,
To tack again each to its lambkin.

This poem has become one of the most easily recognized nursery rhymes. It was almost certainly intended as a simple piece of children's entertainment with the obligatory moral lesson included. In this case, a lesson about responsibility and not, quite literally, falling asleep on the job. The earliest reference to the word is in William Shakespeare's *King Lear*, when the court jester mentions a 'bo peep', which, according to Samuel Johnson's *A Dictionary of the English Language* (1755), means 'the act of looking out and then drawing back as if frightened'.

However, there is a very plausible theory explaining the real meaning behind the words of 'Little Bo Peep'. It starts with Charles I (1600–49). The king had expensive tastes and was keen to dramatically increase the amount of money he received from taxation (see also JACK AND JILL). Needless to say, this proved to be incredibly unpopular and led to frequent run-ins with Parliament, especially when Charles reintroduced an obsolete form of taxation known as 'ship money', insisting on collecting it in peacetime, when this would originally have been authorized only during times of war. Other taxation imposed during this period was an excise tax on essential produce such as grain, vegetables and meat. This, naturally, affected the poor most of all, leading to the Smithfield Riots in 1647 and contributing to the English Civil War in its later stages. Another consequence of higher taxation was the rise in smuggling during this period. All the most secretive coves of southern England were a hive of activity, with ships and boats arriving from mainland Europe loaded with sought-after

(and highly taxed) commodities such as tea, tobacco and
brandy.

And it is down in the small Sussex village of St Leonards,
a picturesque little place where many a smuggling tale is
still told, that we can investigate the claim that 'Little Bo
Peep' was actually a smuggler's tale. To begin with, locals

call one of the Martello Towers in the town to this day 'Bo
Peep'. Records show that the king's customs officers used
the building and regularly imprisoned smugglers in the
cellar before they were transported to London for trial and
probable execution. A nearby minor road is called Bo Peep

Lane, while at the bottom of the lane lies a farm of the same name. It is on a route that leads over the South Downs and to a secluded bay well known for its smuggling connections.

The nearby Bo Peep Public House was a well-known smugglers' den. Smugglers were always more popular along the south coast than the customs men, and locals had a wide network by which they could pass on information, often coded in the form of slang or rhyme. Hence in this context **Little Bo Peep** herself may be seen as the customs men, the **sheep** as the smugglers and the **tails** that had apparently been lost a reference to illicit contraband, such as brandy or rum, being shipped across the English Channel from France.

## Little Boy Blue

LITTLE Boy Blue,
Come blow your horn;
The sheep's in the meadow,
The cow's in the corn.

Where is the boy
Who looks after the sheep?
Under a haystack
Fast asleep.

> Will you wake him?
> Oh no, not I,
> For if I do,
> He will surely cry.

Although the storyline of 'Little Boy Blue' sounds like a romantic reflection of idle country life, there's far more to this rhyme than meets the eye.

The most widely credited theory about its origin is that **Little Boy Blue** is actually Cardinal Thomas Wolsey (*c.*1470–1530), Lord Chancellor and Henry VIII's right-hand man. During his time, Wolsey organized both the affairs of state and the Church with fulsome pomp and ceremony, building the ostentatious Hampton Court Palace for his own use in the process. His extravagance caused so much comment that he was also the subject of another lesser-known rhyme composed in the early 1530s:

> Come ye to court! Which court?
> The king's court or Hampton Court?

Wolsey argued that there was no better place for a visiting nobleman, or even monarch, to arrive in England than on the banks of Hampton Court Palace. The king agreed and duly confiscated Hampton Court for his own use, stripping Wolsey of his office after the latter failed to obtain an annulment of his marriage to Catherine of Aragon. But that is another story (see OLD MOTHER HUBBARD).

During his fourteen years in office, Wolsey commanded

more power than any other Englishman and, though not quite of blue blood (**Little Boy Blue**), he wore the purple robes of a cardinal – the position making him more important even than the Archbishop of Canterbury – and was the Pope's representative in England. His family crest also includes the faces of four blue leopards. Wolsey's high-handed manner earned him many enemies, however, and his tendency to show off, or 'blow his own trumpet', alienated both the nobility and the common people. Also, as the man in charge of the Treasury and the Church, Wolsey was largely responsible for the economically important wool trade (see BAA, BAA, BLACK SHEEP). So the rhyme could well be mocking his fall from grace: **Little Boy Blue** can no longer **blow his [own] horn** now that all his wealth and privilege have vanished away (**The sheep's in the meadow / The cow's in the corn**).

Another contender for Little Boy Blue is Charles II, who, despite being crowned king of Scotland on 1 January 1651, was prevented by Parliament from succeeding his father on to the English throne. Charles tried to make his presence felt by raising an army against England and travelling south but, on reaching Worcester, he was met by Cromwell's forces and soundly defeated. Charles quickly escaped to France where, with a bounty of £1,000 on his head, he kept a low profile for the next nine years. While he was having the time of his life, drinking and gaming at the French and Dutch courts, the early years of the new English Commonwealth were rather less fun, almost every form of entertainment having been banned by the Puritans (see

RIDE A COCK HORSE TO BANBURY CROSS). The rhyme alludes to this period in which the rightful heir (**Little Boy Blue**) peacefully slept away his afternoons while the English nation was in disarray: the sheep would not have been in the meadow and the cows nowhere near the corn if a proper king had been in charge. In other words, England needed her 'shepherd' back.

## Little Jack Horner

LITTLE Jack Horner
Sat in a corner
Eating a Christmas pie;
He put in his thumb
And pulled out a plum
And said, 'What a good boy am I!'

Before the Dissolution of the Monasteries in 1536 there were more than eight hundred religious foundations in England with over 16,000 monks and nuns. During the following five years, they were all seized by the Crown and their land and buildings were either sold off or gifted to supporters of the king. One of the last to go was the ancient Benedictine abbey of Glastonbury and the tale of its own dissolution is said to supply the origin of this rhyme.

The Abbot of Glastonbury at the time was Richard Whyting, a rich and powerful figure who had been a signatory to the First Act of Supremacy (1534) granting King

Henry VIII the legal authority as head of the Church of England. This was an outright rejection of the power of Catholicism and allowed the king to divorce and marry again (see also THREE BLIND MICE).

Despite choosing the king over the Pope, a basic requirement for keeping one's head in sixteenth-century England, Whyting resisted the dissolution of Glastonbury Abbey for as long as possible. It wasn't just that it was one of the wealthiest in the kingdom, it was also a place of huge religious significance.

The abbey was allegedly founded by Jesus's Joseph of Arimathea – the man who donated his tomb for the burial of Christ's body after the Crucifixion – to house the Holy Grail. Joseph is said to have arrived by boat over the flooded Somerset Levels; disembarking at Glastonbury Tor, he stuck his staff into the ground, which flowered miraculously into the Holy Thorn (legend has it that the tree still bursts into blossom every year on Christmas Day). The colourful story was widely believed, Elizabeth I later used it as evidence that Christianity in England pre-dated the introduction of Roman Catholicism, thus legitimizing her role as Defender of the Faith.

So Whyting chose to placate, some might say bribe, the king. He sent his steward, Thomas Horner, to Hampton Court with the deeds to twelve manor houses, concealed beneath the crust of a large pie, posing as a gift. In those days, during property transactions, it was not uncommon for the deeds to be hidden or concealed in transit to ensure they would not fall into the wrong hands, as the actual holder of the deeds was deemed the rightful owner. On the way, legend has it, Thomas Horner delved into the pie and pulled out the deed for a **plum** piece of real estate, Mells

Manor House in the village of Mells, Somerset. And that, apparently, is all he needed to do to become the new lord of that manor.

But the bribe failed and in January 1539 Henry's chief minister, Thomas Cromwell, sent his royal commissioners to Glastonbury to see for themselves what was actually going on down in darkest Somerset. As a result of what they found, Whyting was sent to the Tower of London so that Cromwell could question the abbot in person, and from there he was returned to Glastonbury on 14 November 1539. The following day he was tried for treason, with Thomas Horner as one of the jurors, and found guilty within only a few hours.

That afternoon, Richard Whyting and two of his senior monks, Roger James and John Thorne, were dragged by horses to the top of Glastonbury Tor, where they were hanged, drawn and quartered. Abbot Whyting's head was then displayed above the gates of the deserted abbey as a reminder to others to obey the king without question. Meanwhile Thomas Horner was presumably busy making his removal arrangements.

Unsurprisingly, the descendants of Thomas Horner, who still live at Mells Manor, dismiss the legend as 'pure fantasy

Note: During the 1500s, the slang term for £1,000 was 'plum', just as in modern terms a 'score' is £20 and a 'monkey' £500. Back in the sixteenth century, £1,000 was a seriously large sum of money, as well as being the fixed amount some politicians received for taking on certain government roles. This was considered by the average person as a vast sum of money for doing very little, and that is why these posts became known as 'plum jobs' or 'plum roles'. The expression 'plum' has been used ever since to describe anything of great value that is usually gifted rather than earned.

made up by the Victorians'. Jack's honesty, it is claimed, is supported by John Leland's *Itinerary* (1540–46), a study of ancient buildings and monuments presented to Henry in 1549 that states: 'Mr. Horner hath boute [bought] the lordship of the King.' An alternative account suggests that the king gifted the manor to Horner and that the original title deed, bearing the royal seal, survives in the family's possession to this day.

## Little Miss Muffet

LITTLE Miss Muffet
Sat on a tuffet
Eating her curds and whey.
Along came a spider
That sat down beside her
And frightened Miss Muffet away.

Arachnopohobia is clearly not a modern complaint. Although cobwebs have traditionally been used as a dressing for wounds (and, scientifically tested, have turned out to contain all kinds of antibiotics), spiders have long been seen as malevolent. Richard III, presented by William Shakespeare as the most evil English king, is described as 'a bottled spider', which comes from the belief that spiders were inherently toxic – if one were dropped into a glass of water, every drop would be poisoned. It is therefore entirely understandable that this particular little girl from days gone

by would have been **frightened away** by one, but in fact
there's more to the origins of this rhyme ...

'Little Miss Muffet' first appeared in print in Scotland in
1805, but it was probably around for a long time before
that. Some Scottish historians believe **Miss Muffet** to be
Mary, Queen of Scots (1542–87), and the **spider** John Knox

(*c.*1510–72), the great Protestant reformer and founder of
the powerful Presbyterian Church in Scotland. Knox's best-
known work was *The First Blast of the Trumpet Against the
Monstrous Regiment of Women* (1558) – a notorious attack
against the female Roman Catholic sovereigns of the day, in
particular Mary I of Scotland and Mary I of England, in
which he stated that his purpose was to demonstrate 'how

abominable before God is the Empire or Rule of a wicked woman, yea, of a traiteresse and bastard'. Which goes some way to explaining why he and the young queen were unlikely to see eye to eye, even if she hadn't had such a turbulent and very public love life – twice married, to the French Dauphin (Francis II) and Lord Darnley, both Catholics, and with a purported lover, David Rizzio, murdered by a jealous Darnley. Knox held vast religious influence in Scotland and regularly rebuked Mary, often openly attacking her in his sermons. Eventually her nobles rebelled and she ran away to England, but her cousin Elizabeth turned out to be even less keen on her presence than Knox. Mary was kept under house arrest for nineteen years and then executed. So the Scottish line is that if only Miss Muffet had made friends with the spider, everything could have been so different for her – and for spiders too for that matter.

However, an English interpretation of the rhyme is rather more domestic. Historians point to the eminent English physician Dr Thomas Muffet (1553–1604), staunchly Puritan in his beliefs and therefore close in spirit to John Knox. What he is best known for is his study of insects, particularly spiders, and how they relate to medicine. Hence it is easy to imagine one of Dr Muffet's daughters sitting on a small, three-legged stool (a **tuffet**), eating her **curds and whey** (a dairy product, not unlike cottage cheese), when one of his spiders dropped down and frightened the living curds out of her.

# Little Polly Flinders

LITTLE Polly Flinders
Sat among the cinders,
Warming her pretty little toes.

Mother came and caught her,
And whipped her little daughter
For spoiling her nice new clothes.

The rhyme was first published in 1805 as 'Little Jenny Flinders'. From this we see how **Flinders** is more significant than either **Polly** or 'Jenny' simply because it rhymes with **cinders** and thus ties into a whole series of fairy tales of the rags-to-riches variety. In each case, the beautiful and generally motherless heroine is oppressed by evil relatives and hidden away in the kitchen, her beauty disguised with soot and dirt, in order that someone else (usually an ugly sister) can steal her happy ending.

One of our most famous fairy stories (from a different 'Mother Goose' collection, that of the French writer Charles Perrault – see the Introduction) shows this clearly, Cinderella's very name indicating the dirt she's covered in. Like Polly, and indeed any aspiring princess, she needs clean and beautiful clothes to snare her Prince Charming and get out of the kitchen.

Unlike the story, however, the nursery rhyme is a cautionary tale, warning ordinary little girls not to dream of themselves as fairy-tale figures; that they need to keep their clothes clean because no fairy godmother is going to magically fix things for them and because, if they don't, Mama will go mad and they'll be for it.

# Little Tommy Tucker

LITTLE Tommy Tucker,
Sings for his supper;
What shall he eat?
Brown bread and butter.
How will he cut it
Without any knife?
How will he marry
Without a wife?

In medieval times, it was common for travelling musicians and wandering minstrels to sing, dance or play tunes to a packed tavern in return for a bite to eat and a few jars of stout. The expression 'singing for your supper', already proverbial, would have become even better known after 1829, following the first publication of 'Little Tommy Tucker'. Regarded by most as a gentle children's nursery rhyme, the lyrics actually poke fun at the unfortunate orphans – for whom the name **Tommy Tucker** was a colloquial term – who were often reduced to singing, or begging, for their food. The rhyme also refers to the desperate situation of orphans in the days before the welfare state

– with no status, possessions, family or people who wanted to be associated with them. And little likelihood, therefore, of improving their lot (**How will he marry / Without a wife?**).

# London Bridge Is Falling Down

LONDON Bridge is falling down,
Falling down, falling down;
London Bridge is falling down,
My fair lady.

Take a key and lock her up,
Lock her up, lock her up;
Take a key and lock her up,
My fair lady.

How will we build it up,
Build it up, build it up?
How will we build it up,
My fair lady?

Build it up with wood and clay,
Wood and clay, wood and clay;
Build it up with wood and clay,
My fair lady.

Wood and clay will wash away,
Wash away, wash away;
Wood and clay will wash away,
My fair lady.

Build it up with bricks and mortar,
Bricks and mortar, bricks and mortar;
Build it up with bricks and mortar,
My fair lady.

Bricks and mortar will not stay,
Will not stay, will not stay;
Bricks and mortar will not stay,
My fair lady.

Build it up with iron and steel,
Iron and steel, iron and steel;
Build it up with iron and steel,
My fair lady.

Iron and steel will bend and bow,
Bend and bow, bend and bow;
Iron and steel will bend and bow,
My fair lady.

Build it up with silver and gold,
Silver and gold, silver and gold;
Build it up with silver and gold,
My fair lady.

Silver and gold will be stolen away,
Stolen away, stolen away;
Silver and gold will be stolen away,
My fair lady.

Set a man to watch all night,
Watch all night, watch all night;
Set a man to watch all night,
My fair lady.

Suppose the man should fall asleep,
Fall asleep, fall asleep?
Suppose the man should fall asleep,
My fair lady?

Give him a pipe to smoke all night,
Smoke all night, smoke all night;
Give him a pipe to smoke all night,
My fair lady.

The Romans constructed the original London Bridge out of **wood and clay** in the year AD 60, paving the way for the expansion of Londinium to the south of the River Thames. However, after the Romans left 350 years later, the bridge fell into disrepair (**wood and clay will wash away**). It was first rebuilt in stone in the twelfth century (**Build it up with bricks and mortar**).

There was a long-held pre-Christian belief that burying someone in the foundations of important buildings meant that their spirit would magically protect the structure. For a building as vital to the success of London as the bridge, this could well have made sense. Variations of 'London Bridge Is Falling Down' exist in many other European countries, telling similar tales about their own famous bridges. In fact, when Bridge Gate in Bremen, Germany, was demolished during the nineteenth century, it is said that the skeleton of a child was discovered sealed inside the foundations. So there is every chance the **fair lady** who is **locked into** the bridge in the second verse of the rhyme is the virgin who, legend has it, was secretly buried beneath the bridge during the building work in the twelfth century. As the protective spirit, she is called upon throughout the poem as the person who will know what is best for the bridge.

By the mid 1300s, over 140 shops and houses had been constructed upon the bridge and most of them were used for international trading, especially of gold and silver, as those traders would locate their businesses close to the river in order to trade with the importing merchants docking their ships nearby. This is probably why the reference to **silver and gold** is used in the rhyme, suggesting that it could have been composed at any point between 1300 and 1666 (before the Great Fire), although this particular verse may well have been added to the original text as the bridge, and the goings-on upon it, developed over the years.

In 1666, London Bridge somehow managed to survive the Great Fire of London although some of the arches and foundations were badly damaged. Nevertheless it remained in use until 1758 when the houses and some of the arches were removed as traffic increased along the river. The final verse of the rhyme has clearly been added during the seventeenth century, as pipe smoking was unknown in Europe before Sir Walter Raleigh brought tobacco back from Virginia – along with the potato.

A favourite story to do with London Bridge concerns the newer Victorian model. It was famously bought at auction in 1968 for $2,460,000 by American oil baron Robert P. McCulloch, who had it dismantled and shipped via the Panama Canal to Arizona, where he had it reconstructed, brick by brick, so that it stands today as the world's largest antique. The story goes that the American had, in fact, been fooled into thinking he was buying the more famous landmark of Tower Bridge, often called London Bridge by clueless tourists. The idea that his workmen might have been piecing together his new bridge, brick by brick, in his back garden only for it to become slowly apparent it was not the splendid London landmark depicted on tea towels and T-shirts the world over was hugely amusing to many.

But sadly that story isn't true. After all, when the old London Bridge was put up for auction, any potential bidder would have carried out feasibility studies and structural surveys before interested parties were invited to tender. Only a complete fool could spend nearly two and a half million dollars on the wrong thing, and oil billionaires do not usually turn out to be village idiots.

But there is another theory altogether concerning this nursery rhyme. Some historians see it as the modern version

of an eleventh-century Norse poem written by Ottar the
Black celebrating King Ethelred's use of London Bridge to
conquer the occupying Viking forces in 1014. Ethelred
arranged for his close ally, King Olaf of Norway, to sail his
fleet along the Thames and attach his ships to the wooden
structure of the bridge. As the tide turned, his boats sailed
and the bridge was simply towed away. The two kings then
stormed the Danish stronghold and London was liberated
from Viking rule. But see for yourself:

> London Bridge is broken down,
> Gold is won, and bright renown;
> Shields resounding,
> War horns sounding,
> Hildur shouting in the din!
> Arrows singing,
> Mailcoats ringing –
> Odin makes our Olaf win!
>
> King Ethelred has found a friend,
> Brave Olaf will his throne defend;
> In bloody fight
> Maintain his right,
> Win back his land
> With blood-red hand,
> And Edmund his son upon his throne replace –
> Edmund, the star of every royal race!

Edmund, the son of Ethelred, succeeded his father as king
of England on 24 April 1016. Unfortunately, the **star of**

**every royal race** died later that year, so the celebrations were somewhat premature.

## London's Burning

LONDON'S burning, London's burning,
Fetch the engines, fetch the engines;
Fire, fire, fire, fire!
Pour on water, pour on water.

'London's Burning' is a round, a musical composition in which two or more voices sing exactly the same melody (and may continue repeating it indefinitely), but with each voice beginning at different times so that different parts of the melody coincide in the different voices, but nevertheless fit harmoniously together. (See also FRÈRE JACQUES and TURN AGAIN, WHITTINGTON.)

The song is usually associated with the Great Fire of London of 1666. But in fact there have been many serious fires in London, beginning in AD 61 when Queen Boudicca and the Iceni tribe torched the place after chasing the Romans out of town. The flames were so fierce that the ashes formed a thick layer that can still be clearly identified by modern archaeologists.

'London's Burning' is a relentlessly circular song that could go on for ever, reflecting the frequent fires that have engulfed parts of the capital. And of all the famous landmarks of London that have regularly been caught up in the conflagration, St Paul's, first built in AD 604 on Ludgate Hill, has been the most frequent victim. In 675, a major fire broke out, destroying most of the town, including the Saxon cathedral of St Paul's, largely constructed of wood. It was rebuilt in stone between 675 and 685, then destroyed by the Vikings in 961. A rebuilt St Paul's was, yet again, destroyed by fire in 1087 during the reign of William Rufus (see WHO KILLED COCK ROBIN?).

There were more destructive fires in the capital in 1130 and 1132, while in 1212 the Great Fire of Southwark destroyed large parts of the town. In 1561, the cathedral was burned after being struck by lightning, although the rest of London remained undamaged until the Great Fire in 1666 ravaged everything in its path, including the unfortunate cathedral yet again. In a later century, there was another kind of threat. During an air raid on 12 September 1940, the last time London was ablaze thanks to the hostilities of the Second World War, a German bomb with a delayed timing device hit the cathedral. The bomb might easily have destroyed St Paul's had it not been for the bravery of Temporary Lieutenant Robert Davies, who risked his life to successfully defuse it. Davies was later awarded the George Cross for his actions. Clearly God is not a fireman, but he may be a bomb disposal expert – or a helper of bomb disposal experts.

# Lucy Locket

LUCY Locket lost her pocket,
Kitty Fisher found it;
Not a penny was there in it,
Only ribbon 'round it.

The words to this rhyme involve real people living in
London during the mid 1700s and the tune was later more
famously used as the melody for another song (see YANKEE
DOODLE DANDY). The real **Lucy Locket** was apparently a
London barmaid working at the famous Cock Inn in Fleet
Street during the eighteenth century, while the song itself,
far from being a simple children's rhyme, clearly challenges
her virtue and suggests that she had a second job in another
'profession' – the oldest one of all.

The story goes that one of Lucy's lovers (**her pocket**) had
run through all his funds and consequently found himself
out of favour with the young barmaid. It is said that he
then took up with **Kitty Fisher** (d. 1767), a well-known
courtesan – painted by Joshua Reynolds and encountered
by Casanova, who refused to sleep with her, however, as
she spoke only English whereas he 'liked to have all [his]
senses, even that of hearing, gratified'. She took in Lucy's
cast-off lover, despite his lack of wealth, and then taunted
Lucy for her meanness. Kitty's claim that she had found
a **ribbon 'round** him was a regular insult in catfights of the
day because common prostitutes were known to keep their

money tied to an upper thigh with a ribbon. So one of our most famous children's rhymes is not the innocent ditty that it first appears but a sordid exchange between two ladies of easy virtue.

## The Man in the Moon

THE man in the moon
Came tumbling down
And asked his way to Norwich;
He went by the south,
And burned his mouth
While supping cold plum porridge.

For centuries, people have seen in the surface of the moon either a face or the shape of a man, traditionally believed to be carrying a bundle of sticks and with a little dog at his side. Quite why, in the rhyme, he wanted to go to Norwich is anybody's guess – clearly he didn't know any other towns that rhymed with **porridge**. And quite why he should burn his mouth on something cold is another conundrum – one intended to amuse a child audience.

According to Western folklore, one Sunday, a long time ago, an old man went into the woods with his dog to collect firewood. Having gathered enough sticks, he slung his bag over his shoulder and began the trudge home. Before long, he met a man, who stopped him and said, 'It is Sunday. Don't you know that all good Christians should be resting from their work today?' The old man laughed and replied, 'Sunday on earth, Monday in heaven, it is all the same to me.' The man, a good Christian himself, was outraged: 'Then bear your burden for ever. As you do not value Sunday on earth, then every day will be a moon day for you. You shall stand for eternity in the moon as a warning to all Sabbath breakers.' With that, the man banished the old fellow to the moon, along with his dog and his bundle of sticks.

Though perhaps most famous for writing the hymn 'Onward, Christian Soldiers', Victorian folksong collector, vicar and all-round eccentric Sabine Baring-Gould (1834–1924) was obsessed with the moon and listed all kinds of references to the man supposed to inhabit it. In one version of the story, for instance, the man is carrying willow boughs. In another, he is a sheep stealer who entices sheep with cabbages. Baring-Gould also recounts how the nursery rhyme of JACK AND JILL derives from a Norse legend, in which the moon kidnaps two children, Hjuki and Bil. According to this theory, the figure that we see in the moon is Jack (Hjuki); Jill (Bil) is also there, but less easy to make out. The names 'Hjuki' and 'Bil' mean 'creation' and 'destruction', reflecting the waxing and waning of the moon.

In China, the man in the moon is called Wu Kang; believed to have angered his teachers with his impatience, he was sent to the moon in punishment. In Japan, he is known as Gekkawo, the god of love, who ties lovers' feet together with an invisible cord. Shamans believe they have the power to ascend to the moon and communicate with the old man – without explaining why none of them ever have, mind you. To the Inuit in Alaska the man in the moon is the keeper of all souls, while in Malaysia he is said to be sitting under a banyan tree plaiting a fishing line. A rat keeps chomping through the cord, but this is a good thing as the rat knows that if the old man ever finishes making his line then the world will end.

Back here on earth, scientists have established that the moon is not perfectly round: on one side there is a vast bump in the surface and on the opposite side a giant crater. They believe that it must have been hit by a huge asteroid many millions of years ago. It is the resultant fractures and defects in the moon's surface that have created the shadowing effect interpreted by our ancestors as the silhouette of an old man carrying home some firewood, with his little dog alongside.

# The Man of Thessaly

THERE was a man of Thessaly,
And he was wondrous wise;
He jumped into a thorn bush
And scratched out both his eyes.

And when he saw his eyes were out,
He danced with might and main,
Then jumped into another bush
And scratched them in again.

Thessaly (Thessalia) is the central section of mainland Greece. Surrounded by high mountain ranges encircling a low plain, it borders Macedonia to the north, Sterea Ellada to the south and Epirus to the west, while its eastern shoreline is on the Aegean. The district was the legendary home of the ancient Greek gods and of the Centaurs.

According to Greek legend, a mortal, Bellerophon (**a man of Thessaly**), was given the task of slaying the fire-breathing monster Chimera – a fearsome beast indeed, with its lion's head, goat's body and serpent's tail. For this he used the services of an untamed flying horse called Pegasus and his first job was to subdue the winged steed. Before long, Pegasus was saddled and harnessed and Bellerophon was off to slay the monster.

Assisted by his flying horse, the Greek won many more battles from the saddle, but as his fame grew, so did his arrogance. With so many victories notched up, he felt he deserved a place on Mount Olympus, home of the gods, and this presumption infuriated Zeus, the leader of the gods. As a lesson to the young pretender, Zeus sent a gadfly to sting Pegasus, who threw Bellerophon from the saddle and into a **thorn bush** where he was blinded (he **scratched out both his eyes**). Destitute and crippled, Bellerophon spent the rest of his life stumbling around and seeking a way to reverse his cruel fate. Unlike the hero of the nursery rhyme – who comically **scratched** his eyes in again – he never did.

# Mary Had a Little Lamb

MARY had a little lamb,
Its fleece was white as snow;
And everywhere that Mary went,
The lamb was sure to go.

It followed her to school one day,
Which was against the rule;
It made the children laugh and play
To see a lamb at school.

And so the teacher turned it out,
But still it lingered near,
And waited patiently about,
Till Mary did appear.

Why does the lamb love Mary so?
The eager children cry;
Why Mary loves the lamb, you know,
The teacher did reply.

The imagery and names used in this poem point to its having been constructed as a Christian homily for children. Such rhymes were extremely popular in the eighteenth and nineteenth centuries, so popular, in fact, that William Blake used the form as a template for his famous *Songs of Innocence and of Experience*, published in 1794 (think of 'Little Lamb, who made thee' and 'Tiger, tiger, burning bright'). **Mary**, of course, is the name of Christ's mother and one of the most commonly used images for Jesus is that of the **Lamb** of God, the fleece as **white as snow** a symbol of his goodness and purity. The poem can be read as a parable of Christ's enduring love for mankind (**Why does the lamb love Mary so?**), that he is with Christians everywhere (**And everywhere that Mary went, / The lamb was sure to go**) and that the true Christian should love God and ignore other people's mockery (**It made the children laugh and play**). In the style of these homilies, the teacher would have used Mary's story explicitly to draw this improving moral, spelt out in the final verse. But there's more to the story than that.

To see how the poem came about, we need to go back to the early nineteenth century. It was reported in a 1902 edition of the *New York Times Book Review* that when Dr Lowell Mason introduced singing into Boston schools in 1827 he asked noted writers to contribute songs and rhymes, and one of the contributors was Sarah Josepha Hale (1788–1879), who supplied 'Mary Had a Little Lamb'.

The rhyme proved so popular that many found it hard to believe that it wasn't based on a true incident; indeed Mrs Hale had hinted as much. When in 1913 the *New York Times* ran an interview with Richard K. Powers of Lancaster, Massachusetts, who was celebrating his one hundred and eighth birthday, he talked about 'Mary Had a Little Lamb' and commented: 'Mary was my cousin, her full name was Mary Elizabeth Sawyer.' Very conveniently,

Mary Sawyer had written a complete account, at the age of eighty-eight. Here's her story, in her own words – I've done

a little pruning to keep her to the point because, as you'll see, she's not one for saying things briefly:

> One cold, bleak March morning, I went out with father to the barn and found a lamb that had been born in the night. It had been forsaken by its mother and through neglect was about dead from the cold and for want of food. I saw it had a little life and wanted to take it into the house, but father said no as it was about dead anyway and could only live for

a short time. But I could not bear to see the poor little thing suffer so, and I teased until I got it into the house and then worked on mother's sympathy.

At first it could not swallow, and the catnip tea I had mother make, it could not take for a long time. I got the lamb warm first thing, which was done by wrapping her in an old garment and holding her in my arms beside the fireplace. All night long I nursed the lamb and at night it could swallow just a little.

In the morning, much to my girlish delight, it could stand and then improved rapidly. It soon learned to drink milk, and from the time it could walk about it would follow me anywhere if I called it. It was a fast grower, as symmetrical a sheep who ever walked and its fleece was of the finest and whitest. Why, I used to take as much care of it as a mother would of a child. I used to wash it regularly, keep the burdocks out of its feet and comb and trim with bright coloured ribbons the wool on its forehead. And when that was being done, the lamb would hold down its head, shut its eyes and wait as patiently as could be.

Then my brother Nate said: 'Let's take the lamb to school with us.' When the schoolhouse was reached, the teacher had not arrived but a few scholars were there. I took her down to my seat – you know we had the old-fashioned, high-boarded seats back then. Well, I put the lamb under the seat on a blanket and she lay down just as quietly as could be.

By and by, I had to get up to recite and left the lamb all right, but in a minute there was a clatter, clatter on the floor and I knew it was the pattering of the hooves of my lamb. Oh, how mortified I felt. The teacher laughed outright and of course all the children giggled. It was rare sport for them but I couldn't find anything mirthful in the situation. I was too embarrassed and ashamed to even laugh or smile. I took the lamb out and put it in the shed until I was ready to go home at noon, when it followed me back.

Visiting the school that forenoon was a young man called John Roulstone. He was very pleased at the school incident and the next day he rode across the fields on horseback, came to the little old schoolhouse and handed me a slip of paper which had written on it three verses, which are the original lines, but since then there have been other verses added by a Mrs Townsend.

Personally, I have a few doubts. In the first place, if the lamb was so special to Mary, why didn't it have a name? And if it did have a name, why didn't she use it, or how had she forgotten it and yet remembered so many other small details so many years afterwards? Also, the rhyme was not published until 1830, fourteen years later. Would you still remember something a passing nine-year-old had written about your pet all those years ago?

While there may be some dispute about whether Roulstone wrote any part of the poem, or whether Sarah Hale composed the whole thing, Massachusetts has nonetheless claimed the rhyme (and the consequent increase in their tourist industry), and both Mary Sawyer's house in Sterling (until it burned down in 2007) and the small Redstone

School have been preserved as a memorial. Today, in Sterling town centre, there stands a statue of a lamb in tribute to John Roulstone and displaying the first verse of the poem. Incidentally, Mary Sawyer's little lamb, a ewe, apparently lived to be four years old and had three of her own baby lambs.

Personally, I prefer this version of the rhyme:

> Mary had a little lamb,
> It really was a glutton;
> It quickly grew into a sheep
> And ended up as mutton.

Or this one:

> Mary had a little lamb,
> But then she had a hunch
> When Dad came home with mint sauce,
> They were having lamb for lunch.

# Mary, Mary, Quite Contrary

> MARY, Mary, quite contrary,
> How does your garden grow?
> With silver bells and cockle shells
> And pretty maids all in a row.

This nursery rhyme, with its innocent-sounding verse and the charming picture it evokes, has been happily recited by children for hundreds of years, none of whom are likely to have known about its strange, much darker origins. There are three theories about the background to the rhyme. It's basically a case of choose your own Mary: either Mary I of England (1516–58), Mary, Queen of Scots (1542–87), or, more controversially, the Virgin Mary.

The first explanation refers to Mary I's turbulent reign (see THREE BLIND MICE). When her father severed links with the Catholic Church to divorce her mother, it led to a deep rift between the king and his daughter. Mary was banished from court and sent away to live under virtual house arrest at the Palace of Beaulieu in the Essex farmlands.

Henry's son, King Edward VI (Mary's younger half-brother), succeeded his father and pursued his Protestant reforms with even greater enthusiasm than Henry. As the first English king of the Protestant faith at the time of his coronation, Edward felt he had the work of God on his hands and even drafted the 'Device to Alter the Succession', removing his half-sisters, both the moderate Protestant Elizabeth and the devout Catholic Mary, from the line of succession in favour of his solid Protestant cousin Lady Jane Grey. He knew that Mary, if allowed to succeed him, was going to be one contrary queen.

Mary did succeed him, however (after the reign of Lady Jane, the 'Nine Days' Queen', which was the shortest in English history), and her first action as queen was to order the release of the prominent Catholics Thomas Howard and Bishop Steven Gardiner from the Tower of London.

Gardiner had once been a staunch ally of both her father and half-brother but, after refusing to renounce his faith, made an enemy of the powerful Thomas Cranmer. Mary then set about reversing all the religious legislation of her predecessors, plunging England into turmoil (**Mary, Mary, Quite Contrary**). Steven Gardiner was appointed Bishop of Winchester and Lord Chancellor. Almost all other privy counsellors had opposed Mary's accession to the throne and so Gardiner, whom she regarded as her only real supporter and confidant, was given the honour of crowning the new queen on 1 October 1553. Hence for **garden** in line 2 of the rhyme, we should read 'Gardiner'. Another possible variation on this line associates gardens with graveyards – 'How does your graveyard grow?' – reflecting the growing number of dead Protestants in the aftermath of Mary's accession. It has also been suggested that the 'garden' and all that grows in it may be a taunting reference to Mary's empty womb – her failure to produce a Catholic heir (see FLOUR OF ENGLAND).

During Mary's bitter purge of the Protestants, Gardiner ordered imprisoned dissenters to be tortured using a gruesome array of devices, including instruments known as **cockleshells** for crushing a person's genitals, thumbscrews called **silver bells** and rows of early guillotine-type devices used for beheading, known as 'maidens' or **maids**.

The second theory identifies the Mary of the rhyme as Mary, Queen of Scots, who certainly had a chequered and somewhat contrary career herself (see LITTLE MISS MUFFET). When she sought refuge in England with her cousin Elizabeth, she was immediately put under house arrest. As a former queen, she lived in luxurious surroundings, but she was also under constant scrutiny. **How does your garden grow?** is therefore a sarcastically posed question in this context. She had exchanged her kingdom for a suite of rooms in various fortified stately homes, after all. Nonetheless, she remained a focus for all the closet Catholics (**cockleshells and silver bells** are symbols of Catholicism) and rebellious thinkers in Elizabethan England, and represented a constant danger to the throne. Despite this, Elizabeth was reluctant to deal harshly with a sister queen. In the end, however, Mary's contrariness was her own downfall when she was implicated in a plot to depose Elizabeth. She was executed on 8 February 1587, at Fotheringhay Castle in Northamptonshire.

And, last but not least, this rhyme can also be read as an allegorical description of Roman Catholicism, central to which is worship of the Virgin Mary, one of whose titles is even *hortus inclusus*, the walled **garden**, celebrating her virginity. Although the second line of the rhyme could equally well be seen as a Protestant taunt, reminding the Catholics that their sphere of influence wasn't actually growing any more. **Cockleshells** were worn on the hats of Catholic pilgrims, **silver bells** gave the summons to worship, and **pretty maids all in a row** were the nuns who forswore marriage in favour of duty to the Church. So, as I said, just pick your own Mary . . .

# Monday's Child

MONDAY'S child is fair of face,
Tuesday's child is full of grace,
Wednesday's child is full of woe,
Thursday's child has far to go.
Friday's child is loving and giving,
Saturday's child works hard for his living,
And the child that is born on the Sabbath day
Is bonny and blithe and good and gay.

The origins of this rhyme come from the ancient belief that each day of the week has something special about it. Even today that can be seen very clearly in the names of our weekdays. Sunday was the day of the sun and Monday of the moon. The rest of the week comes from the Norse gods: Tuesday is named after Tyr, the god of single combat; Wednesday after Woden, the one-eyed king of the gods; Thursday after Thor, the god of war; and Friday after Freya, the goddess of love. Saturday is the day of Saturn, the Roman god of farming. Depending on what day of the week you were born, you would come under the protection of its particular deity and hence your character would reflect theirs.

This is reflected in the rhyme: Saturday's child **works hard for his living**, toiling in the fields or at a desk; Sunday's child is sunny-natured (**bonny and blithe and good and gay**); Monday's is good-looking (as proverbially **fair** as the moon); and Friday's appropriately **loving and giving**. When it comes to the remaining days of the week, the rhyme goes its own way, however. Children born on a Tuesday, Wednesday or Thursday would otherwise be a pretty feisty lot, if not downright bolshy and apt to pick a fight. They'd be dealing out **woe** rather than on the receiving end of it.

On that very point, the rhyme has long bothered many who were born on a Wednesday. I have even read about one poor soul who convinced himself he was born on a Tuesday instead. And then there is the woman who booked a Caesarean on a Tuesday to make sure her daughter wasn't saddled with the implications of a Wednesday birthday for the rest of her life. Well, I have good news for all of those whose lives have been ruined by finding out they were born on a Wednesday. Because the original publication of the rhyme in *Harper's Weekly* on 17 September 1887 went like this:

> Monday's child is fair of face,
> Tuesday's child is full of grace,
> Wednesday's child is loving and giving,
> Thursday's child works hard for a living,
> Friday's child is full of woe,
> Saturday's child has far to go;
> But the child that is born on Sabbath-day
> Is bonny and happy and wise and gay.

So that is good news, isn't it? Unless you were born on a Friday, in which case I'm sorry about that.

# Needles and Pins

NEEDLES and pins,
Needles and pins,
When a man marries,
His trouble begins.

**Needles and pins** (or, as we more commonly say these days, 'pins and needles') is the tingling or pricking sensation you get when you've been sitting or lying in one position for too long and your foot or hand goes numb. There are no long-term effects – which makes it unlike marriage, the rhyme's argument goes, where prickliness can last a lifetime.

This is a traditional rhyme, thought to have been written about Henry VIII and his troublesome wives, although arguably it should be the other way round as we all know that it was his wives for whom **trouble** began when they married the king. Except for Catherine Parr, of course, who managed to outlive him.

Needles and pins of a literal kind were one of the smaller (if still sharply pressing) problems Henry VIII encountered during his reign. At the time, most of them were made in the monasteries, so when their factories were closed down following the Dissolution of the Monasteries (see LITTLE JACK HORNER and SING A SONG OF SIXPENCE), a huge vacuum was created in the marketplace. Pins and needles became very expensive and the king tried to rectify the problem by passing an act in 1543 encouraging industry of the day to manufacture more of them. The importance of pins, due to their relative scarcity, is reflected in this rhyme:

> See a pin and pick it up,
> All the day you'll have good luck;
> See a pin and let it lay,
> Bad luck you'll have all the day.

## Old King Cole

> OLD King Cole was a merry old soul,
> And a merry old soul was he;
> He called for his pipe,
> And he called for his bowl
> And he called for his fiddlers three.
> Every fiddler he had a fiddle
> And a very fine fiddle had he;
> Oh, there's none so rare as can compare
> With King Cole and his fiddlers three.

Some believe that the rhyme must have been written after the introduction of tobacco to Europe in 1564. But it goes back much further, to the early part of the first millennium where the **pipe** was actually much more likely to have been the double aulos, an ancient reed instrument, and the **bowl** a type of drum favoured by wandering minstrels and entertainers. In addition, the word *coel* is the Gaelic word for 'music', so could **Old King Cole** be the 'Old King of Music',

the venerable leader of a band, playing the pipe and drum
with his **fiddlers three**? Or could he have been a real person?
Digging further, we find three possible candidates for him.

The first, Coel Godhebog (otherwise known as Coel the
Magnificent), was Lord of Colchester (believed to be Latin
for 'Coel's Fort') and lived in the third century AD. This

was the period of the Roman occupation of Britain and
Coel was a decurion, responsible for running local affairs.
The emperor of the western Roman Empire at the time was
Flavius Valerius Constantius (250–306), and legend has it
that he went to Britain in 296 to consolidate Roman inter-
ests. Here he fell in love with Coel Godhebog's daughter,
Helena, and became Coel's successor, their son growing
up to become Constantine the Great. While it is entirely

possible that Constantius fell in love with Coel's daughter, it is unlikely she was Constantine the Great's mother. Especially as Constantine was actually born twenty years earlier, around 272, in another part of the empire – his mother was indeed a Helena (famed for her piety, she later became St Helena), but a Bithynian rather than a Briton. However, the Romans had certainly perfected the art of a party by the end of the third century, with or without pipes and fiddles, so was Coel the Magnificent the real Old King Cole?

Or was it Coel Hen (350–420), also known as Coel the Old as he lived for seventy years (an unusually long time in the days when there was always a war to fight or a disease to catch)? Coel the Old was also Lord of Colchester, at the time of the decline of the Roman Empire. In fact, Hen is thought to have been the final decurion as the last of the Romans fled the country under pressure from the barbarians. Hen, though, remained and fought long battles in the north of England against the Picts and the Scots.

Finally, we have his son, St Ceneu ap Coel, who was born in 382. He also remained in Britain and is thought to have been elevated to saintly status after defending Christianity against the pagan onslaught. Hugely popular, St Ceneu later became king of northern Britain. In his *History of the Kings of Britain* (1136), Geoffrey of Monmouth lists St Ceneu as a guest at the coronation of King Arthwys, his grandson. In the past, many historians have believed that Arthwys, born around 455 and who became the king of southern Wales, was the inspiration for the legend of King

Arthur. So which King Cole is the rhyme about, the Magnificent, the Old or the Saint? Or could it be an amalgam of all three?

A thousand years later, the first of the Tudor kings, Henry VII (1457–1509), insisted he descended from King Cole (not specifying which one) in order to strengthen his own claim to the throne, but this claim is almost impossible to prove as most of the information on record about England's ancient kings was gathered many centuries after the event and hence based on legend, fable and handed-down stories.

## Old Mother Hubbard

OLD Mother Hubbard
Went to the cupboard
To fetch her poor dog a bone.

But when she got there
The cupboard was bare
And so the poor dog had none.

She went to the fishmonger's
To buy him some fish,
But when she came back
He was licking the dish.

She went to the grocer's
To buy him some fruit,
But when she came back
He was playing the flute.

She went to the cobbler's
To buy him some shoes,
But when she came back
He was reading the news.

For the origins of this rhyme we need to go back to the sixteenth century, to a prominent figure from this unique period in history, when religious and political sagas dominated the English way of life. Criticizing the rich and powerful – especially the monarch and the Church – was a dangerous pastime that could lead at best to a day in the stocks, where ill-wishers would come along and pelt you with stones or rotten vegetables, and at worst to being hanged, drawn and quartered or burned alive. Anonymously penned rhymes in the guise of nonsense verse for children therefore provided a safe means of letting off steam while also relaying vital information. Some historians believe Old Mother Hubbard's cupboard is meant to represent the Roman Catholic Church, with all the power and resources that particular organization had at its disposal, while the Old Mother is Cardinal Wolsey (c.1470–1530), one of the most important and powerful churchmen of the sixteenth century, and at one time a close ally of King Henry VIII.

According to this interpretation, when Henry asked for a divorce from his first wife, Catherine of Aragon (see MARY, MARY, QUITE CONTRARY and THREE BLIND MICE), he sent **Old Mother Hubbard** (Cardinal Wolsey) to the Vatican (the **cupboard**) to obtain a **bone** (the divorce scroll) for the **dog** (the king himself). But, on finding that the **cupboard was bare** (the Vatican wasn't going to sanction a divorce), Wolsey fell from favour with the king, who took his newly built palace at Hampton Court from him and rejected the Catholic Church into the bargain. The **poor dog** might not have got his bone but he became definitely much richer in the process.

But how do verses three, four and five fit into all this? For that we need to dig a little further into the history of the rhyme. The earliest publication of the poem was in 1790, as 'The Adventures of Mother Hubbard and her Dog', credited to one Sarah Catherine Martin (1768–1826), a British writer responsible for twelve other popular works on Mother Hubbard. It is claimed that a real Mrs Hubbard was housekeeper at Kitley House, Yealmpton, in south Devon where Sarah was a regular guest. But this is just hearsay, unfortunately, as there is no mention of either Sarah Martin or Mrs Hubbard in any of the very detailed literature about Kitley. The old Mother Hubbard, in this case, appears to be entirely fictitious.

In any case, the earliest reference to 'Old Mother Hubbard' dates back much further, to 1591, making it entirely possible that both suggested origins could be true. After all, the complete nursery rhyme does give the impression of being two separate poems welded together. The first two verses are very different from the remaining section in terms of construction (four lines instead of three), and the vocabulary of the first part seems simpler and older in style. So there is a strong indication that the first two verses were written at a much earlier date than the rest and could quite easily be about Henry VIII and Wolsey, while the remaining stanzas could have been added by Sarah Martin to give more colour to her series of adventures involving her favourite old lady and dog. At least, that is what I conclude from all this.

## Oranges and Lemons

ORANGES and lemons,
Say the bells of St Clement's;
You owe me five farthings,
Say the bells of St Martin's;
When will you pay me?
Say the bells of Old Bailey;
When I grow rich,
Say the bells of Shoreditch;
When will that be?
Say the bells of Stepney;
I do not know,
Says the great bell of Bow;
Here comes a candle to light you to bed,
And here comes a chopper –

To chop off your head!
Chip chop, chip chop –
The last one is dead!

This rhyme is usually sung by children as a party game. Two will start the game off by facing each other and holding hands to form an archway, or 'chopper'. The others will then form a line and as they all sing the rhyme they pass under the arch. On the last word, the 'chopper' will catch the child passing though and he or she is then out of the game. Interestingly, this points towards the grim events that underlie this seemingly innocuous rhyme. But first a bit of history.

While the earliest traceable written record of the rhyme dates to around 1745, there is a dance tune called 'Oringes and Lemons' listed in John Playford's *The English Dancing Master*, first published in 1665. In the nursery rhyme, the bells are all those of London churches. Although some of the churches were damaged by the Great Fire of London in 1666, all of them still stand to this day. The rhyme plots a journey through London, using the churches as landmarks. Let's have a look at each in turn:

### St Clement's Church

London has two St Clement's vying to be the one mentioned in the verse. It could be St Clement's Church in Eastcheap, on the grounds that it is located close to the docks (St Clement was the Roman patron saint of sailors) where cargos of citrus fruit (**oranges and lemons**) often arrived from the Mediterranean. It is recorded that the bells of St Clement's would ring as each ship arrived at the dockside, filled to the gunwales with fruit. The church of St Clement Danes in Westminster would appear to have an equal claim, however, also being situated near the docks. According to Charles Dickens in *The Pickwick Papers* (1836–7), porters, having collected their fruit from the wharf, would use the churchyard as a shortcut and paid a toll to the church in return for carrying their oranges and lemons to Clare Market nearby. St Clement Danes takes this claim seriously enough to play the 'Oranges and Lemons' melody on its bells on a daily basis and each year holds a special 'oranges and lemons' service.

Sadly, though both churches were certainly located in the fruit-trading areas of old London Town, there is little convincing evidence supporting either claim. In any case, all this citrus fruit is really a cover for a much bitterer cargo: condemned men were also unloaded at the docks and then taken through the streets of London to a public execution, the bells of the particular churches ringing their death knell. All of which makes St Clement's in Eastcheap the most likely candidate for the first bell a prisoner would hear.

### St Martin's Church

The first record of the bells of the church of St Martin Orgar dates from 1469, when parish accounts note an expense for 'a rope for ye sauns bell, mending the bell, mending the wheel and a socket for the rope to run in'. The church is located very close to St Clement's at Martin Lane in the City of London, an area formerly well known for its pawnshops and money lenders. Martin Lane is also only yards from Pudding Lane where, famously, the Great Fire started.

A farthing was a fourth of a penny (a 'fourthing', hence 'farthing'), although back in those days five farthings was quite a reasonable sum of money. Returning to our condemned man, it's possible that those who knew him would make a last-ditch attempt to get their money back (**You owe me five farthings**).

### Church of St Sepulchre-without-Newgate (Old Bailey)

St Sepulchre-without-Newgate, the largest parish church in the City of London, is located on Holborn Viaduct, directly opposite the Old Bailey, the central criminal court in England. The clerk of the church, known as the Bellman, was given the responsibility of ringing a hand bell outside the condemned cells at midnight before an execution was due to be carried out, and the following rhyme would be recited through the locked door:

> All you that in the condemned hole do lie,
> Prepare you, for tomorrow you shall die;
> Watch all and pray, the hour is drawing near
> That you before the Almighty must appear;
> Examine well yourselves and in time repent
> That you may not to eternal flames be sent;
> And when St Sepulchre's Bell in the morning tolls,
> The Lord above have mercy upon your souls.

Famous as one of the 'Cockney bells', the great bell of Old Bailey would traditionally be rung to mark the execution of a prisoner at the gallows of the nearby Newgate Gaol. The payment of the debt the prisoner is about to make (**When will you pay me?**) is not in money.

### Shoreditch Church

The bells of Shoreditch are located in the belfry of St Leonard's Church on Kingsland Road. Shoreditch Church, as it is better known, was in an area outside the city wall noted for its extreme poverty and lawlessness. **When I grow rich** would have sounded particularly ironic from the **bells of Shoreditch** and from a man on his way to execution.

### Church of St Dunstan and All Saints, Stepney

The St Dunstan and All Saints Church in Stepney was originally built in AD 952 by Dunstan (909–88), London's favourite saint from the Middle Ages. He was a local boy who became Bishop of London, then Archbishop of Canterbury and then (posthumously, of course) a saint. The **bells of Stepney** were famous for their clear sound and, here, drive the point further home: **When will that be?** It's a question the condemned man can no longer answer.

### Church of St Mary-le-Bow

Known locally as Bow Church, the site of St Mary-le-Bow in Cheapside has had a church upon it since 1080. It is a place long associated with death. In 1340, the population of London was 50,000 but in 1348 the Black Death claimed over 17,000 lives. During this time, the bells at St Mary-le-Bow rang out the curfew each day to keep the ever-diminishing population of the City within its walls and therefore under quarantine. Here the bell provides a pessimistic answer – **I do not know** – to the question posed by the bells of the previous church.

Incidentally, the use of Bow bells as a curfew leads us to an explanation of how 'Cockney' is defined. Each day the bells would ring out at nine in the evening, the signal for everybody to be off the streets and the non-residents away from the City limits. From then onwards it was decided that anybody who could actually hear the bells was an inhabitant of the City, while those who lived in districts where they could not hear the bells were deemed non-residents and not subject to the curfew. This has led to the celebrated claim that anybody considered to be a real Londoner, or Cockney, must have been born within the sound of the Bow bells in Cheapside and not in Bow (a separate district of London), as many East Enders insist.

The Bow bells are also said to be responsible for Richard (Dick) Whittington (1354–1423) 'turning' back to London and to great prosperity and success – eventually becoming London's most famous Lord Mayor (see TURN AGAIN, WHITTINGTON). The message the bells are sending the prisoner in this rhyme is a rather bleaker one, however. They mark the end of his journey (**Here comes the candle to light you to bed**) and they aren't holding out much hope (**Here comes the chopper to chop off your head**). It's rather a chilling discovery that the game we all blithely played as children is in fact a macabre re-enactment of a medieval execution.

## The Owl and the Pussycat

THE Owl and the Pussycat went to sea
In a beautiful pea-green boat;
They took some honey, and plenty of money,
Wrapped up in a five-pound note.
The Owl looked up to the stars above
And sang to a small guitar,
'O lovely Pussy! O Pussy, my love,
What a beautiful Pussy you are,
You are,
You are!
What a beautiful Pussy you are!'

Pussy said to the Owl, 'You elegant fowl,
How charmingly sweet you sing!
O let us be married! too long we have tarried:
But what shall we do for a ring?'
They sailed away, for a year and a day
To the land where the Bong-tree grows
And there in a wood a Piggy-wig stood
With a ring at the end of his nose,
His nose,
His nose,
With a ring at the end of his nose.

'Dear Pig, are you willing to sell for one shilling
Your ring?' Said the Piggy, 'I will.'
So they took it away, and were married next day
By the Turkey who lives on the hill.
They dined on mince and slices of quince,
Which they ate with a runcible spoon;
And hand in hand, on the edge of the sand,
They danced by the light of the moon,
The moon,
The moon,
They danced by the light of the moon.

'The Owl and the Pussycat' has featured in countless books
and been illustrated hundreds of times since its original
appearance in Edward Lear's *Nonsense Songs, Stories,
Botany and Alphabets*, published in 1871. Lear (1812–88)
was a noted author of nonsense verse and credited with
popularizing the art of the limerick. 'The Owl and the
Pussycat' was written in 1867 and presented as a gift to
the children of his patron and benefactor Edward Stanley,
the 13th Earl of Derby. This led to rumours that the real
author was the earl himself as many believed Derby was
using his first name, Edward, plus an anagram of the word
'earl' as a pen name.

The poem is notable for introducing the word **runcible**
into the English language. Indeed, during the 1920s, nearly
four decades after the poet's death, some dictionaries began
defining the word as a small, three-pronged pickle fork,
curved like a spoon and otherwise known as a 'spork'. But

this does not describe the spoon featured in the original illustration of Lear's poem nor, for that matter, the one in his illustration of the 'Dolomphious Duck' in which the runcible utensil, while big enough to hold a frog, is quite clearly a spoon and not a fork. In fact, lexicographers of the 1920s appear to have completely missed Lear's references to the word in other poems, such as a 'runcible cat', 'runcible hat', 'runcible goose' and 'runcible wall'. None of which could possibly have anything to do with the three-pronged spork. Clearly Lear made the word up for his own amusement and for the entertainment of others and yet it sparked off a hunt for the meaning lasting several decades. I'd like to suggest that if any linguistic explorers are still looking for the **Bong-tree** and a ring-wearing **Piggy-wig** they should stop right now.

# Polly Put the Kettle On

POLLY put the kettle on,
Polly put the kettle on,
Polly put the kettle on;
We'll all have tea.

Sukey take it off again,
Sukey take it off again,
Sukey take it off again;
They've all gone away.

One popular theory about the origins of 'Polly Put the Kettle On' centres on the life of a writer living in London in the mid eighteenth century with his young family of two boys and three girls. Apparently there were many arguments between the children about who could play in which room of the house. The girls, keen to be rid of the noisy boys, would often pretend to start a girls-only tea party. The youngest, Polly, would reach for the toy kettle as the other girls sang: 'Polly put the kettle on.' At this point, the boys would scarper, leaving the girls to play quietly together in the drawing room as the eldest girl, Susan, took the kettle back off again. (**Polly** was a common pet-form of 'Mary', as was **Sukey** of 'Susan', in middle-class families of the time.) Their father was so enamoured with the girls' cheek that he wrote it all down, set it to music and the rhyme was subsequently published. It is a charming story, although there is little evidence of this actually ever having happened.

However, this is what we do know. Joseph Dale originally published a poem called 'Molly Put the Kettle On' in 1809 and shortly afterwards 'Molly' was substituted with 'Polly' in a version published in Dublin. The melody is similar to a rather strange 1788 Viennese folksong called 'O du lieber Augustin' ('Oh, you poor Augustin'), about a popular street musician who, in 1679 as the bubonic plague tore through Vienna, fell into a pit filled with plague victims while making his drunken way home one evening. Luckily, Augustin managed to crawl back out and, somehow, also avoided catching the disease.

'Polly Put the Kettle On' was hugely popular in the nineteenth century. Grip, the raven in Charles Dickens' *Barnaby Rudge* (1841), when very much excited cries, 'Hurray! Polly put the kettle on, we'll all have tea; Polly put the kettle on, we'll all have tea. Hurrah! hurrah! hurrah!' 'Polly put the kettle on and we'll all have tea' became a popular catchphrase at Victorian tea parties, the precursor to 'Shall I be Mother?'.

# Poor Old Robinson Crusoe

POOR old Robinson Crusoe!
Poor old Robinson Crusoe!
They made him a coat
Of an old nanny goat;
I wonder how they could do so!
With a ring a ting tang,
And a ring a ting tang,
Poor old Robinson Crusoe!

Robinson Crusoe is the hero of Daniel Defoe's *The Life and Strange and Surprising Adventures of Robinson Crusoe*, a book based upon the true experiences of one Alexander Selkirk, who had run away to sea in 1695 to avoid a court summons in Scotland for 'indecent behaviour in church'. (The mind boggles.) In 1704, after correctly judging the ship he was sailing on to be unseaworthy, Selkirk deserted on the uninhabited Pacific island of Más a Tierra, only to find himself stranded there for nearly five years, although he would later discover that his former ship had indeed foundered at sea and most of his crewmates had drowned. Selkirk was finally rescued in 1709. Then, in 1719, English author Daniel Defoe published his own version of the story (often described as the first novel in English), to great acclaim. Crusoe is a rather more appealing character than Selkirk – he's shipwrecked rather than a deserter, for instance. He stays on the island for twenty-three years longer than his real-life counterpart and has all kinds of adventures, including run-ins with cannibals. The book has been a children's favourite ever since its first appearance.

The nonsense rhyme has much more to do with the iconic pictures associated with the book – where Crusoe is always shown dressed in a homemade fur garment (**They made him a coat / Of an old nanny goat**) – than the text itself. It paints a very light-hearted picture of Crusoe's experiences; he was kept company by goats but had no human companion (or not until he rescued Man Friday several years into his stay). In another triumph of fiction over fact, in 1966 the island that had been home for Selkirk for so long was officially renamed Robinson Crusoe Island while another nearby took the name Alejandro Selkirk Island.

# Pop Goes the Weasel

HALF a pound of tuppenny rice,
Half a pound of treacle.
That's the way the money goes,
Pop goes the weasel.

Up and down the City Road,
In and out the Eagle.
That's the way the money goes,
Pop goes the weasel.

Every night when I go out,
The monkey's on the table.
Take a stick and knock it off,
Pop goes the weasel.

A penny for a ball of thread,
Another for a needle.
That's the way the money goes,
Pop goes the weasel.

There has been much debate over the years about the meaning of 'Pop Goes the Weasel'. A hugely popular music-hall song, its memorable and seemingly nonsensical lyrics spread like wildfire throughout Victorian London. But is there more to the rhyme than meets the eye?

For centuries, the poor and immigrants had lived outside

the walls of the City of London in Spitalfields, Hoxton and Shoreditch. These were traditionally areas of high crime and even higher poverty. Ever since the arrival of the Huguenots, French Protestant refugees escaping religious persecution in the 1680s, it had been where all London's textile work and weaving took place. Packed with sweatshops, it was also the epicentre of the thriving entertainment business and the site of many music halls and theatres whose audiences consisted of the local workers who did long shifts in the factories or laboured in their own homes, creating clothes for very low wages.

One theory suggests that 'Pop Goes the Weasel' was an attempt to turn the grim reality of local people's lives into a hit song. In the textile industry, a spinner's **weasel** was a mechanical thread-measuring device in the shape of a spoked wheel that accurately measured out yarn by making a popping sound to indicate the correct length had been reached. The mind-numbing and repetitive nature of the work is captured in the final line of each verse, indicating that whatever you were doing, or wherever your mind had wandered to, reality was never far away with the weasel to **pop** you alert again. The rest of the lyrics can be seen as snapshots of mundane, everyday life in Shoreditch – of having enough money to buy food (**rice** and **treacle**), spend on visits to the **Eagle** music hall on **City Road,** or pay for the tools of the trade (**A penny for a ball of thread, / Another for a needle**). That was the way the money went.

A more recent theory involves Cockney rhyming slang – invented by East Enders wishing to communicate only with their own kind. Here set phrases are used to indicate an object that rhymes with the final word, hence 'apples and pears' for 'stairs' or 'frog and toad' for 'road'. Which is reasonably straightforward once you get the hang of it,

although you have to be a bit quicker on the uptake when just the first part of the phrase is used, as in 'He fell down the apples' or 'I'm going down the frog'. In rhyming slang, **weasel** comes from 'weasel and stoat' and means 'coat'.

So, according to this interpretation, the rhyme tells the

story of an East End pub crawl (**Up and down the City Road, / In and out the Eagle**). The current Eagle pub (which has the words of the nursery rhyme painted on its wall) on the **City Road** is the site of the former Royal Eagle Tavern music hall. A **monkey** was a sailors' term in Victorian times for the glazed jug or tankard they drank their rum and grog rations from. 'Knocking off a stick' meant to drink alcohol. This raucous night out used up every penny of the worker's wages (**That's the way the money goes**), leaving nothing to live on for the rest of the week.

It would have been a hand-to-mouth existence at the best of times. In those days, many people relied on the pawn-broker, who would advance money against objects that were left with him. Many would have to put their **weasel** into pawn (**pop**), in order to be able to buy even the cheapest and nastiest food (**Half a pound of tuppenny rice, / Half a pound of treacle**) to keep themselves going until the next payday. After all, without a coat or money, they weren't going to be able to go on another bender **up and down the City Road** for the time being. Although it's a dark song, it also catches the happy-go-lucky attitude that saw one good night out as worth a week surviving on tuppenny rice and treacle, and the people it was written about easily identified with it.

The earliest published version of 'Pop Goes the Weasel' appeared in America during the early 1850s. American news sheets labelled it 'the new English dance', while, back in England, *The Times* published an article in 1853 describing various popular songs and dances of the day, including

'La Tempête, La Napolitenne and Pop Goes the Weasel, three celebrated dances'. In 1854, Boosey & Co., a well-established music and book shop in London, included the following words in one of their adverts: 'The new country dance "Pop Goes the Weasel", introduced by Her Majesty Queen Victoria', suggesting that the rhyme had now reached a wider audience – from East End music hall to Royal Variety Performance.

# Punch and Judy

PUNCH and Judy fought for a pie,
Punch gave Judy a blow in the eye;
Says Punch to Judy, 'Will you have more?'
Says Judy to Punch, 'No, my eye is too sore.'

Traditionally performed at seaside towns and other holiday resorts, although also making appearances at country fairs and markets, Punch and Judy shows originated in Italy during the early part of the seventeenth century. It was the commedia dell'arte who first introduced the character Punchinello to their popular street theatre.

The first appearance of Mr Punch was in England on 9 May 1662 (considered by enthusiasts to be his official birthday), introduced by Italian puppeteer Signor Bologna, and the anarchic comedy character was an immediate success. Soon afterwards, the diarist Samuel Pepys watched a performance in Covent Garden, London, and noted 'an

Italian puppet play ... which is very pretty. The best I have ever seen and a great resort of gallants.'

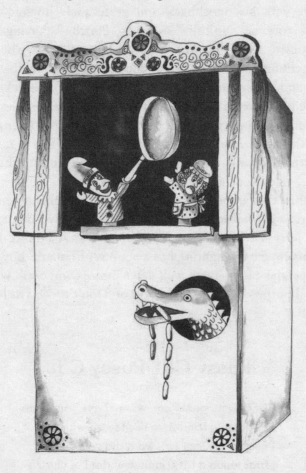

In the British version of the show, the cast usually consists of Punch, his wife Judy (originally called 'Joan'), their baby, a crocodile, a policeman and a string of sausages. Dressed in a jester's costume, Punch strikes a distinctive figure with his hunchback and grotesquely hooked nose. The storyline typically involves Punch behaving outrageously, struggling with his wife Judy and the baby, and then triumphing in a series of encounters with the forces of law and order (and often the supernatural). Knockdown comedy has remained wildly popular ever since (show an audience a character being beaten about with a frying pan or other such implement and they'll laugh their heads off) and the stick that Punch wields so freely is in fact thought to provide the origin of the term 'slapstick'.

When the puppets hit each other, it's like the violence in a cartoon – indeed, Punch and Judy probably taught Tom and Jerry a trick or two – and they always bounce back. In this rhyme the fighting has a serious aftermath, however. Hence the poem may well have been composed with a moral purpose – an early version of 'Don't try this at home, kids!'

## Pussy Cat, Pussy Cat

PUSSY cat, pussy cat, where have you been?
I've been to London to see the queen;
Pussy cat, pussy cat, what did you there?
I frightened a little mouse under her chair.

This short rhyme has been popular since the reign of the last Tudor monarch, Queen Elizabeth I (1533–1603). For once, this is a story without a dark origin. The rhyme is said to have evolved from a tale told by one of the Virgin

Queen's ladies-in-waiting. It is believed that an old, fat tomcat used to roam the corridors of Windsor Castle and nobody knew where he came from or where he was going. But one day the lazy cat lay down to sleep under the queen's great throne (**her chair**) and slept throughout an entire royal audience.

Waking suddenly with a jolt and surprised to hear so

much noise, the cat made a bolt for freedom between the queen's legs, nearly frightening her majesty to death. Amid the fuss, one of the courtiers grabbed the animal and returned it to the queen for punishment. But the great lady took pity and passed a royal order that the cat's life would be spared and the little fellow was free to roam the castle in return for chasing away the rats and mice. If it is a true story – and I do hope so – it may well have also inspired the adage that a cat may look at a king.

# The Queen of Hearts

THE Queen of Hearts
She made some tarts,
All on a summer's day;
The Knave of Hearts
He stole the tarts
And took them clean away.

The King of Hearts
Called for the tarts
And beat the Knave full sore;
The Knave of Hearts
Brought back the tarts
And vowed he'd steal no more.

The first known appearance of this rhyme in print is in 1782. Contrary to appearances, it isn't about a kitchen theft, but tells a nursery-rhyme version of a game of cards. The **Queen, Knave** and **King of Hearts** are all cards, while the **tarts** are the winning points passed from player to player until the game is won.

But how we read this rhyme today is coloured by the interpretation of mathematician and keen card-player Lewis Carroll in his classic work *Alice's Adventures in*

*Wonderland* (1862). Backed up by John Tenniel's equally influential illustrations – which immortalized HUMPTY DUMPTY as an egg – she is clearly a caricature of Britain's eccentric and autocratic monarch of the time, Queen Victoria, with elements of the real person to make her at once instantly recognizable to parents reading the story to their children, but fantastical enough to render her unrecognizable to children. In *Alice in Wonderland*, the King of Hearts (like Prince Albert) is meek and compliant, while his wife, the Queen of Hearts, is clearly very much in charge. But Carroll's queen is also based on the history of the playing card itself. The original Queen of Hearts first emerged on a deck of playing cards produced in France in 1650, apparently inspired by the Old Testament figure of Judith. When all seemed lost for the Jewish people, this beautiful (if steely) woman had managed to take Holofernes, the evil Assyrian general, off guard and cut off his head.

In a mocking echo of the biblical story, Carroll's queen is completely obsessed with decapitation: 'The Queen had only one way of settling all difficulties, great or small. "Off with his head!" she said, without even looking round.' During the trial of the Knave (for stealing the tarts), virtually every witness is in danger of losing his or her head, Alice included.

# Rain, Rain, Go Away

RAIN, rain, go away,
Come back another day;
Little Johnny wants to play.
Rain, rain, go to Spain,
Never show your face again.

A favourite with little children, this rhyme originated
during the reign of Queen Elizabeth I when the English
were at war with Spain. In 1588, the Spanish sailed their
fleet of over 130 ships to attack the English coastline. The
Anglo-Spanish Wars between 1585 and 1604 were fuelled
by a deep-rooted rivalry between the two countries that had
escalated during the discovery of the New World, namely
North and South America and the West Indies, as both
battled for control of the new trading routes.

The English vice-admiral, Sir Francis Drake, is famous
for his insistence on completing his game of bowls when
the Armada was sighted, but he knew the weather was
worsening and waited until the right moment to launch the
smaller, faster English fleet. The English ships' captains,
better used to the unpredictable weather in the English
Channel, made use of the howling gales and lashing rain
of the great storm and routed the advancing Spanish ships,
scattering them in all directions and then hounding them
south (**Rain, rain, go to Spain, / Never show your face
again**).

Incidentally, the name **Johnny** has often been used as a derogatory term for an Englishman and, to this day, the English are referred to in some parts of the world as 'Johnny English' or 'Johnny Englander'. This is also why so many other nursery rhymes and patriotic songs include either the name Jack or John, as these were taken to mean any Englishman. In the rhyme, the name is used to demonstrate how the English nation was tired of fighting the Spanish.

# Red Sky at Night

RED sky at night,
Shepherd's delight;
Red sky in the morning,
Shepherd's warning.

In the Middle Ages, production of wool and other textiles formed the backbone of the English economy (see BAA, BAA, BLACK SHEEP). Which is why shepherds and their flocks regularly appear in some of our oldest rhymes. Long before twenty-four-hour weather forecasting, country folk relied upon clues from nature to predict forthcoming weather. According to such country lore, birds will build their nests high in the branches of a tree during the spring if their instinct informs them the coming summer will be warm and dry and they therefore don't need to rely on the shelter afforded by the lower branches. Cows lying down in a meadow are a sure sign of rain as instinct instructs them to keep the ground beneath them dry, while haze around the moon at night is another indication of rain to come. Bees will remain in their hives if a storm is coming, while high-flying swallows indicate warm, dry weather ahead.

In a similar vein, shepherds – who spent all their working day outside and, like farmers in general, needed to be able to predict bad weather as their livelihood depended on it – grew to recognize that when there was a particularly red sunset then the following day would be bright, clear and sunny. However, a **red sky** at sunrise usually indicated stormy, inclement weather for the day ahead. And it appears that meteorology can back up the folklore. The reason the sky glows red is due to the sun shining on the underside of clouds from a low angle, either at sunrise or sunset. As weather systems generally move from west to east, this reflection would predict, with reasonable accuracy, if rain clouds were moving towards you in the morning or away from you during the night.

# Remember, Remember the Fifth of November

REMEMBER, remember the fifth of November,
Gunpowder, treason and plot;
I see no reason why gunpowder, treason
Should ever be forgot.

Guy Fawkes, Guy Fawkes, it was his intent
To blow up the King and the Parliament;
Three score barrels of powder below,
Poor old England to overthrow.

By God's providence he was catch'd
With dark lantern and lighted match;
Holler boys, holler boys, make the bells ring,
Holler boys, holler boys, God save the King.

Living in our high-tech world, it is difficult to imagine a
time when it was impossible to link up to the planet at
large, and everyone on it, at the touch of a button or a
single click of a mouse. It is only seventy years since the
cinema, followed by television, began to bring news to
the select few. Events reported were two days old but that
was instantaneous compared with former times. After
the Battle of Trafalgar in 1805, for instance, nobody in
England knew about the great victory, or Nelson's death,
for months.

So think back to the year 1605, a time when very few people could read and the only news of national importance would be when King James's army turned up at your remote farm to recruit men for yet another war in God's name. Many lived their entire lives in blissful ignorance of the wider world. James I was the first monarch of the new dynasty (reigning from 1603 to 1625) and hence his position was rather less stable than he would have liked – as a celebrated attempt on his life only two years into his rule was to prove. His government had to find a simple and effective way of delivering its message to the far corners of the land, as quickly as possible. And as most country folk could neither read nor write, this would have to be done by word of mouth. An easily memorable rhyme or limerick would do the trick admirably – encapsulating important news and, in this case, providing a stern warning in just a few snappy lines.

So when Robert Catesby led his gang of religious terrorists – thirteen men, including the hapless Guido (Guy) Fawkes – in the most famous failed terrorist attack in English history, the king needed to make sure all of his subjects were made aware of the dastardly plot and warned against entertaining similar ideas.

Catesby's gang had planned to blow up the Houses of Parliament on the first day of the new session on 4 November 1605: the king and many other powerful Englishmen would have been killed at a single stroke. The idea was to incite rebellion and restore a Catholic head of state by putting King James's nine-year-old daughter Elizabeth on the throne. Catesby's plan was to pack the cellars of the Houses of Parliament with as much gunpowder as could be smuggled in. One of the men, Guy Fawkes, an explosives expert, would hide in the cellars all night long and then light a fuse to explode the barrels as soon as the king and his court were sitting directly above the cellars the following day.

But a member of the gang tipped off a family friend due to attend the opening of Parliament and that friend informed the authorities. Fawkes was caught, quite literally, with his hand on the fuse and the assassination attempt was foiled. A recent television re-enactment of the Gunpowder Plot has proved that, had it been successful, it would have certainly wiped out most of the great and good of the English ruling classes. During the re-enactment, the resulting controlled explosion was so severe that the head of the mock king was blown to the other side of the River Thames. Condemned for high treason, Guy Fawkes's body parts could likewise be found all over London after their owner had been hanged, drawn and quartered. His mutilated body was displayed as a deterrent to others and a warning of the seriousness of treason. His head was placed on a pike at the Tower of London where the ravens pecked his skull clean.

The following year, a sermon was commissioned by Parliament to commemorate the foiling of the plot and the survival of the monarchy, and an annual custom was thereby established. The prominent clergyman Lancelot Andrewes (co-compiler of the King James Bible) first read the sermon and then recited the verse to be remembered and repeated as worshippers returned to their towns and villages throughout England. That year, loyal townsfolk formed lamplit processions in honour of the king and built huge fires on which they burned effigies of the conspirators in what was to be repeated as an annual reminder of what happens to those who commit treason and threaten the monarchy. Fireworks were later introduced to replicate the explosion that might have taken place. Such bonfires were normal at the time, with effigies of England's 'enemies' burned on a regular basis at village greens throughout the land, although these days, thanks to 'Remember, Remember the Fifth of November', it is specifically the Gunpowder Plot of 1605 that is never forgotten.

Children soon began a tradition that has continued ever since of stuffing old clothes with paper and hay and displaying their flammable models of Guy Fawkes on street corners, asking passers-by for a penny for their efforts. 'A penny for the guy, mister?' became a familiar cry, although the last street urchin I passed asked for a fiver, demonstrating once again how times have changed.

# Ride a Cock Horse to Banbury Cross

RIDE a cock horse to Banbury Cross
To see a fine lady upon a white horse;
With rings on her fingers and bells on her toes,
She shall have music wherever she goes.

Some argue there can only be one historic figure who could inspire such a rhyme. Step forward Lady Godiva, England's favourite naked horsewoman. During the eleventh century, England was divided into four great provinces – Wessex, East Anglia, Mercia and Northumbria – each governed by an earl. In 1040, according to legend, Leofric, the Earl of Mercia, tried to impose heavy taxes on his countrymen, provoking outrage and near riots. Leofric's wife, Godgifu (changed over time to Godiva), sympathized with the common people and urged her husband to lower the new taxes he had levied.

Now, Leofric was obviously a man with a sense of humour because he told his wife he would lower taxes only after she had ridden naked through the streets of Coventry. But he hadn't reckoned upon Godiva's spirit and, much to his surprise, she agreed to the challenge. The delighted people of Coventry, as a show of respect, all agreed to stay indoors, close their shutters and face the other way as the lady passed by, to spare her blushes. She rode through the streets on her beloved **white horse**, completely naked apart from her wedding ring (**rings on her fingers**), and with **bells** attached to her toes to remind the people of Coventry not to look out of their windows. All the citizens kept their word,

except for Tom the tailor, who couldn't help himself and peeped out through the shutters. According to legend, Tom was then struck blind – hence the expression 'peeping Tom'.

But if it's a rhyme about Lady Godiva, surely the town mentioned in the rhyme should be Coventry? If we turn to the town of Banbury, in Oxfordshire, we encounter another horse-riding lady, Celia Fiennes, sister of the 3rd Viscount Saye and Sele of Broughton Castle, Banbury. According to this account, for **fine lady** we should read 'Fiennes lady'. However, while the location is right and everything seems to fit quite nicely, it appears that the story is suspect – probably concocted by a member of the Fiennes family.

**Banbury Cross** is genuine, though. Indeed, Banbury once had three historic crosses: the White Cross, the High Cross and the Bread Cross, all important religious symbols in the settlement that was located on top of a relatively steep hill. Which brings us to our third lady on horseback ...

This theory relates to the day Queen Elizabeth I travelled through Banbury on one of her annual progresses through the kingdom. In keeping with the fashion of the era, the Virgin Queen wore fine **rings** on her fingers and soft velvet shoes with **bells** sewn into the fabric. On reaching Banbury Hill, her carriage broke a wheel, leaving her entire entourage stranded outside the town.

Luckily, Banbury had **a cock horse** to hand. This is an old carriage-driving term, referring to an extra (male) horse employed to assist pulling a cart or carriage up a steep hill. As was common at the time, the town's council provided traders with the free use of the horse, to help carts laden with goods make an easy passage into town. Banbury's officials soon came to the rescue, Elizabeth mounted the cock horse, decorated with ribbons and more bells for its royal passenger, and rode through the town to the cheers of her delighted subjects (**She shall have music wherever she goes**).

This is all very charming and colourful but the rhyme is much more likely to have arisen from a rather darker episode in Banbury's past. In the early sixteenth century, the town became a hotspot for Puritan zeal. (Even today the local football team, Banbury United FC, are known as 'The Puritans'.) During the English Civil War, under the aegis of local MP Sir Anthony Cope, a group of one hundred and fifty men converged upon the town and destroyed the famous medieval crosses as part of the Parliamentarian edict to remove anything that might smack of idolatry. To the hardline Puritans, the rich and much decorated Catholic Church, decked out in all its finery like a beautiful woman (**rings on her fingers and bells on her toes**), was the 'Whore of Babylon'. The Banbury crosses represented part of this finery, and must be destroyed to make way for Protestant plainness. It was hardly surprising that after the Parliamentarians had won the war they went on to ban any form of entertainment, whether it was morris dancing, football or just a drink down the pub. They even cancelled Christmas. (The name of the modern football team must be entirely ironical, therefore.)

# Ring-a-Ring o' Roses

RING-a-ring o' roses,
A pocketful of posies;
A-tishoo! A-tishoo!
We all fall down.

This rhyme usually accompanies a dancing game that ends with all the children falling to the ground, getting their clothes muddy and going home to a clout round the ear. Or at least that's how I remember it.

'Ring-a-Ring o' Roses' is traditionally associated with the plague – the Great Plague of London in 1665 or the Black Death of the late 1340s – and it is easy to see why. A plague victim would show early symptoms of the disease in the form of red, circular rashes all over the body resembling wreaths of roses (**Ring-a-ring o' roses**). The rhyme also seems to reflect the superstition that if a person was to carry around a pouch, or 'pocket', stuffed with herbs or 'posies', there was less chance of infection (**A pocketful of posies**). Sneezing would be also be a symptom (**A-tishoo! A-tishoo!**), indicating that the person was in an advanced state of infection, certain to **fall down** (dead) very shortly afterwards. So far so neat.

Unfortunately this doesn't actually accord with the known symptoms of the disease. Between two and six days following infection, the illness becomes obvious in a person. The early signs are headaches, chills, high fever. No rosy rings. Following the fever would come the formation of buboes, an inflammatory swelling of the lymph glands in both the groin and armpits. There is no historical record that posies, herbs or any other flower were used as preventive medicine, although there is evidence that sweet-smelling

flowers were sometimes carried to counter the terrible odours in areas affected by disease. (People were so terrified of catching the plague, in fact, that they are known to have resorted to extreme measures – burning all their clothes, possessions and sometimes even their houses in the hope of avoiding infection.) And finally, there is no reference anywhere to sneezing as a final and fatal symptom of the plague.

One of the strongest arguments given for the rhyme being connected with the plague is, in fact, one of the strongest arguments against it. Several historians have urged in favour of the association. But the big question is this: if indeed the rhyme dates as far back as the Black Death in the 1340s, then why did nobody write it down for over five hundred years?

No contemporary record of the rhyme has been found from that period. Even Samuel Pepys (1633–1703), the noted diarist and chronicler of a later outbreak, the Great Plague, makes no mention of it, although it seems unlikely that no record should be made until 1881, centuries after it was – seemingly – first sung. In fact, no connection had been made between 'Ring-a-Ring o' Roses' and either of the plagues until 1961, when James Leasor proposed the idea in his book *The Plague and the Fire*.

In conclusion, while the connection between rhyme and plague makes a good story, it appears far more likely that 'Ring-a-Ring o' Roses' is a simple children's party game, illustrating nothing more than a group holding hands in a circle and dancing around, to the accompaniment of satisfying sounds effects (**A-tishoo! A-tishoo!**) and actions (**We all fall down**). In its first publication in Britain, in 1881 – in Kate Greenaway's *Mother Goose* – the sneezing wasn't even part of the rhyme, perhaps suggesting a later addition:

> Ring-a-ring-a-roses,
> A pocket full of posies;
> Hush! hush! hush! hush!
> We're all tumbled down.

The version in Alice Gomme's *Dictionary of British Folklore* (1898) reads:

> Ring a ring of roses,
> A pocket full of posies;
> Upstairs, downstairs,
> In my lady's chamber.

While, as late as 1949, a version included in a collection of verse entitled *Poems of Early Childhood* – illustrated with four happy children dancing in a circle and carrying bunches of roses – still carries no reference to the fatal sneezing:

> Ring a ring a rosy,
> A pocket full of posies;
> One, two, three, four,
> We all fall down.

## Rock-a-Bye, Baby

ROCK-a-bye, baby, on the tree top,
When the wind blows the cradle will rock;
When the bough breaks the cradle will fall,
And down will come baby, cradle and all.

Also known as 'Hush-a-bye, Baby', this lullaby has several theories concerning its origins. One tells us that the words relate to the Glorious Revolution of 1688 that led to the downfall of King James II of England (see THE GRAND OLD DUKE OF YORK). It has been suggested that King James's son was secretly replaced at birth, without his knowledge, by another baby in order to provide a true Catholic heir. Such are the lengths people would go to for religious purposes. The breaking **bough** in the rhyme is said to be the rotten Stuart monarchy, while the **wind** is supposed to represent the wind of change blowing in from the Nether-lands in the shape of James's Protestant nephew, William of Orange, who could provide a genuine Protestant monarchy once again in England. Finally, the **baby** is England herself – in dire peril from the conflict between these two opposing forces.

Another argument may in the end owe more to simple English myth or legend. During the mid eighteenth century, a family lived in a great yew tree at Shining Cliff Woods in Ambergate in Derbyshire. The tree was over a thousand years old and the family occupying its branches were the local charcoal-burners Kate and Luke Kenyon. With the permission of the wood's owners, the Hurt family, the Kenyons hollowed out a cradle in one of the huge branches for the youngest of their eight children. The Hurts were apparently so fond of the Kenyons that they are said to have commissioned the artist James Ward to paint their portrait. But this picture does not exist, unfortunately, and checking the dates shows that Ward (1769–1859) was far too young to have painted them, making the entire tale highly unlikely, albeit very charming.

A popular theory from America is that a descendant of the great American folk hero Davy Crockett, Effie Crockett (1857–1940), composed the song as a fifteen-year-old in 1872 while looking after a baby and trying to rock it to sleep. However, as the first printed record of the lullaby can be traced to 1765, when it was published by John Newbery, a children's book specialist in London, this appears to rule out that claim. And various other theories about the rhyme's purported English origins don't hold much water either. One suggests that it was written by the 3rd Earl of Sandwich, Edward Montague, heartbroken after his son was accidentally tipped from his cradle into the River Thames and drowned in 1706. This sounds even less likely, however, on discovering that his only son, Richard Montague, lived until he was thirty.

The most convincing theory is in fact American and harks back to the sixteenth century. Reputed to be the first English language poem ever written on American soil, the rhyme is believed to have been penned by a young English pilgrim who had travelled to the New World in 1621 on the *Mayflower*. He had observed the way in which Native Wampanoag Indian mothers of Massachusetts crafted cradles out of tree bark and suspended them from the branches with vines, placing their offspring inside and thus allowing the soft wind to rock the babies to sleep. However, he also added a darker note with his warning (aimed at the Pilgrim Fathers, and Mothers, who might be trying out this method with their restless children) that sometimes the vine or branch could snap.

# Rub-a-Dub-Dub

> RUB-a-dub-dub,
> Three men in a tub,
> And how do you think they got there?
> The butcher, the baker and candlestick maker,
> It was enough to make a man stare.

This is one of those nursery rhymes that we all take for granted. When looked at again, it's a very much odder affair. At first glance, 'Rub-a-Dub-Dub' looks rather like a reference to a gay peep show. Indeed, history reveals that there probably was such a thing, catering especially for royalty and the nobility. There is every chance the working classes also had their own clandestine man-on-man entertainment going on in towns and cities throughout the land. However, the oldest printed version of the rhyme, dating to the fifteenth century, reveals how changing just a few words can alter a story completely, putting an entirely different complexion on it:

> Rub-a-dub-dub,
> Three maids in a tub,
> And who do you think were there?
> The butcher, the baker and candlestick maker,
> And all of them gone to the fair.

Peep shows were popularized by the Victorians during the nineteenth century, but their origins can be traced back much further, to Europe in the 1400s. In those days, wandering artists and entertainers came up with the idea of presenting their art or shows in a large portable wooden box. The inside could be decorated to create scenery and customers would pay to watch the action through holes in the side. It was all innocent fun in the beginning but soon developed into the perfect way of providing 'closet' sexual entertainment for the public without breaking too many laws. That was probably when those Victorians became so interested in them.

# See-Saw, Margery Daw

SEE-SAW, Margery Daw,
Johnny shall have a new master;
He shall earn but a penny a day
Because he can't work any faster.

See-saw, Margery Daw,
Sold her bed and lay on straw;
Was not she a dirty slut
To sell her bed and lie in the dirt?

See-saw, Margery Daw,
The old hen flew over the malt house;
She counted her chickens one by one,
Still she missed the little white one,
And this is it, this is it, this is it.

This song has been sung by children, past and present, as they play on a see-saw, its rhythm mimicking the rising and falling motion of the see-saw itself. And like so many rhymes, there's more to it than first meets the eye. A see-saw in a metaphorical sense brings the low high and high low, and thus this rhyme explores what happens when family situations change for the worse.

The first verse clearly refers to child labour, something that up until the mid nineteenth century was completely taken for granted. When Charles Dickens's father was imprisoned for debt in 1824, the middle-class twelve-year-old had to leave school and work ten-hour days in a boot-blacking factory to support his family. Resentment of his situation and the conditions under which working-class people lived became a major theme in his later works. Whatever age you were, if you were poor you had to work. It is quite possible that the rhyme was used as a taunt to other children: that if they failed to work at a harder and faster rate, they would be sent to the workhouse, where life was guaranteed to be even worse for them than it was up the chimney or out in the fields.

The second verse takes the next step and is about poverty, destitution and perhaps even prostitution. After all, no young girl willingly sells her bed to lie on straw. The second half of the verse is about society's negative reactions to sudden poverty (**Was not she a dirty slut/To sell her bed and lie in the dirt?**); no one helps, they just point the finger.

The third verse then takes a step back and looks at the family missing its 'lazy' child – the one who **can't work any faster.** They are no longer part of the community, perhaps sent to the workhouse (**the malt house**), where they are scorned by society – emphasized by the singer of the rhyme suddenly pointing at the child being taunted (**And this is it, this is it, this is it**). Altogether, not a very pleasant little song.

# Simple Simon

SIMPLE Simon met a pieman,
Going to the fair;
Said Simple Simon to the pieman,
'Let me taste your ware.'

Said the pieman to Simple Simon,
'Show me first your penny.'
Said Simple Simon to the pieman,
'Sir, I have not any.'

Simple Simon went a-fishing,
For to catch a whale,
All the water he had got
Was in his mother's pail.

Simple Simon went to look
If plums grew on a thistle;
He pricked his fingers very much,
Which made poor Simon whistle.

He went to catch a dicky bird,
And thought he could not fail
Because he had a little salt
To put upon its tail.

> He went for water in a sieve,
> But soon it all fell through,
> And now poor Simple Simon bids
> You all a simple 'Adieu'.

At first glance, this seems like straightforward nonsense verse, but in fact the figure of Simple Simon is a very ancient one – arising from the old Christian idea of the holy fool. 'Fools for Christ', a phrase first used by St Paul, refers to behaviour motivated by real or assumed craziness, to serve a religious purpose. Such people might employ shocking, unconventional behaviour to challenge accepted norms, deliver prophecies or to mask their piety. According to this interpretation, Simple Simon is trying – and failing – to perform a series of miracles, some of which use the imagery of the Old Testament (poverty, fishing, the carrying out of impossible tasks). Unsurprisingly enough, the patron saint of holy fools was a sixth-century maverick called St Simeon of Ermesa.

Simeon's career as a saint started out with the required years of prayer and study, twenty-nine in all. But his story took a dramatic turn when he left his cave one day and entered the world. His chosen city was Emesa, in Syria, and he started as he meant to go on – much to the bemusement of the people of Emesa – with a dead dog tied to him. And that was only the beginning. During church services, he threw nuts at the clergy and blew out the candles. At the circus, he wrapped his arms around the dancing girls and went skipping across the arena, to the amusement of the masses. In the streets, he tripped people up, developed a theatrical limp, and dragged himself around on his buttocks; while, down in the bath house, he ran naked into the crowded women's section. On solemn fasting days, he ate vast amounts of beans – with noisily predictable results. It is easy to see how, in his lifetime, Simeon must have been regarded as a madman.

It was only after his death that people started to talk about his acts of kindness – and about they had turned into off beat miracles. There was the poor mule driver whose vinegar Simeon turned into wine, enabling him to start a successful tavern. There was the rich man who was saved from death when Simeon threw a lucky triple six at dice. And then there was the young man Simeon punched on the jaw to save him from an affair with a married woman in a literally backhanded act of kindness. Rather than being a madman, St Simeon the Holy Fool wanted the events of his life to show how (in the words of St Paul again) God chooses 'the foolish things of the world to shame the wise; the weak things of the world to shame the strong' (1 Corinthians 1:27).

Simple Simon often appears in the literature of the late Middle Ages, but slowly the imagery connected with him changes and the religious element is dropped in favour of slapstick, plain and simple. This Simple Simon has to suffer because he knows no better; the fool is no longer holy, he just rushes in where angels fear to tread. In this vein, a chapbook ballad published during the later part of the seventeenth century and called *Simple Simon's Misfortune* tells the tale of an unfortunate man whose habit of losing and breaking things causes his wife to be cruel to him throughout their marriage. Meanwhile, another Simple Simon appears as the hero of a story written by Hans Christian Andersen in 1855, although presented more sympathetically. The idiot younger son of a wealthy family, he surprises everybody, including himself, when he somehow wins the hand in marriage of a beautiful princess after his elder, more intelligent brothers have failed.

# Sing a Song of Sixpence

SING a song of sixpence, a pocket full of rye;
Four and twenty blackbirds baked in a pie.
When the pie was opened, the birds began to sing;
Oh, wasn't that a dainty dish to set before the king?

The king was in his counting house counting out his money,
The queen was in the parlour eating bread and honey.
The maid was in the garden hanging out the clothes
When down came a blackbird and pecked off her nose.

This rhyme has been a favourite for centuries and there are a number of stories about it. One story focuses upon Henry James Pye (1745–1831), who was appointed Poet Laureate in 1790. Unfortunately, Pye lacked one significant attribute for the role: he was a terrible poet. One of the first tasks given to him was to write an ode in honour of mad King

George III's birthday. The rhyme, peppered with references
to feathered choirs and vocal groves, was ridiculed by other
writers one of whom, George Steevens, immediately
quipped of the long-awaited effort: 'and when the PYE was
opened the birds began to sing; was that not a dainty dish
to set before the king?' Pye was later described as the worst
Poet Laureate in English history; indeed, his successor,
Robert Southey, once remarked: 'I have been rhyming as
doggedly and dully as if my name had been Henry James
Pye.' But let's get back to the origins of the rhyme ...

Songbirds were once a delicacy in England – and in some
parts of Europe, especially France, they still are. It takes
only a small leap of the imagination to see how food of
days gone by could easily have inspired this rhyme. Royal
meals have always been constructed to impress and, like
showgirls jumping out of cakes, twenty-four live songbirds
bursting out of a huge dish covered with an already-cooked
pastry lid would certainly have wowed even the most jaded
of royal diners. But there's far more going on here than a
banquet.

According to one theory, the **king** in the rhyme was Henry
VIII, the **queen** Catherine of Aragon, his first wife, and the
**maid** Anne Boleyn, his mistress and wife-to-be. Like several
other rhymes, 'Sing a Song of Sixpence' has to do with the
Dissolution of the Monasteries. In those much more dangerous times, it was crucial to transport sensitive documents
around the kingdom in as unobtrusive a way as possible.
Like the title deeds in LITTLE JACK HORNER, they were
sometimes concealed in pies, and many deeds to valuable

properties formerly owned by the Church were gifted to the king by black-clad churchmen (**blackbirds**) looking for a place in government or in Henry's new Church of England. These political schemers used the opportunity to betray their superiors in return for financial reward or status, but they made highly unreliable allies, as Anne Boleyn was to find to her cost. Once she had given birth to a daughter rather than the much desired male heir, they were ranged against her. A plot was fabricated by Thomas Cromwell and the poor girl was accused of adultery, incest and high treason, leading to her head being cut off in 1536 (**down came a blackbird and pecked off her nose**).

A much less likely theory, but my favourite nonetheless, is this one. Long before Johnny Depp and Keira Knightley glamorized piracy, there lived a man called Blackbeard (*c.*1680–1718), king of the pirates. He lived during an age when ships from the great European nations sailed the seas in search of new lands to be plundered and vast riches returned to the ruler who authorized such activities. Ships' captains and their crews could become amazingly wealthy if they returned home safely – a big 'if' as pirates often lay in wait for an authorized vessel to complete its voyage before attacking it as it headed for home, laden with bounty.

Blackbeard operated in and around the Caribbean Islands with a fair degree of success, and before long several nations had put a price on his head. As a result, he kept a low profile when recruiting for new crew at the start of each season's campaign. 'Sing a Song of Sixpence' was his coded message to potential shipmates.

*Sing a song of sixpence, a pocket full of rye*

Blackbeard, unlike many pirate captains, paid his crew a decent daily wage of sixpence per man, thereby attracting the best rogue sailors around. The king of the pirates also offered seamen a **pocket full of rye** whisky a day – a leather pouch holding about a litre of grog – which would have been a big incentive for any sailor, who liked to drown his seafaring sorrows with a liberal dose of alcohol. (Traditionally, almost all of them.)

*Four and twenty blackbirds baked in a pie*

Blackbeard was fond of a springing surprises and one of his tricks, to lure a target vessel close enough, was to pretend his own boat was in distress and in danger of sinking. Sails would be arranged to make the ship appear as though it was in difficulty or had lost its mast in a gale. Honest sailors from passing vessels would then go to the rescue, little realizing that **twenty-four** of Blackbeard's finest drunkards would be lying in wait.

*When the pie was opened the birds began to sing*

As the target ship drew alongside, Blackbeard's **blackbirds** would spring into action, usually with fearsome screams and shouts, jump aboard and quickly overpower the rival crew, killing as many as possible and then forcing those who surrendered to either join their gang or walk the plank.

*The king was in his counting house, counting out his money*

This obviously refers to the pirate king himself. Money was the motivating factor behind his actions. It didn't hurt to remind new recruits how lucrative piracy could be.

*The queen was in the parlour, eating bread and honey*

Blackbeard's favourite ship, *Le Concorde de Nantes*, was stolen from the French navy in 1717. He renamed it the *Queen Anne's Revenge* and probably liked to remind potential recruits of the celebrated theft.

*The maid was in the garden, hanging out the clothes*

A **maid** was pirate slang for a choice ship known to be laden with treasure, while the waters around the Caribbean and Carolinas were referred to as 'the **garden**'.

*When down came a blackbird and pecked off her nose*

Blackbeard's 'birds' always had to be at the ready, and speed was often their best weapon – a surprise attack on a ship to 'peck off her nose' (maids and ships both being feminine) before the crew realized what was happening. All of which explains why 'Sing a Song of Sixpence' could be associated with seafaring 'kings' as much as land-based ones. Although personally I doubt it.

# Solomon Grundy

SOLOMON Grundy,
Born on a Monday,
Christened on Tuesday,
Married on Wednesday,
Took ill on Thursday,
Grew worse on Friday,
Died on Saturday,
Buried on Sunday;
That was the end of Solomon Grundy.

A rhyme used for hundreds of years to teach children the order of the days of the week – and to remind them, cheeringly enough, that life is extremely short – 'Solomon Grundy' was first published in 1842 by researcher and Shakespearean scholar James Orchard Halliwell-Phillips. The name **Solomon Grundy** is believed to derive from a popular dish known as Salmagundi. Originating in the early seventeenth century, this consisted of a variety of ingredients, including cooked meats, seafood such as anchovies and pickled herrings, salad leaves and dried fruits. Washington Irving used the name of the dish as the title of a literary magazine, issued from January 1807, in order to emphasize the publication's eclectic mix of articles and with the intention of poking fun at New York's politics and culture. Incidentally, it was in the pages of *Salmagundi* that Irving first nicknamed New York as Gotham City, an Anglo-Saxon word meaning 'Goat Town' – which is how I see the place, but that's another story.

The number seven is regarded as significant by many different cultures and religions. In Genesis, in the Old Testament, God creates the world in six days and then rests on the seventh. In Roman Catholicism, there are other sacred sevens, but the one most relevant to this rhyme is the seven sacraments. These are the special ceremonies performed at different stages in a person's life: baptism, Eucharist or Mass, reconciliation (including confession), confirmation, marriage, taking holy orders, and anointing of the sick (or last rites). Clearly not all these apply to our Mr Grundy (he wasn't a monk, for instance, and clearly didn't have much time to commit any sins, let alone confess them), but a set of sacraments is nonetheless implied – those significant stages in every person's life.

'Solomon Grundy' isn't the only traditional rhyme to show a life in a week. There's also this one:

Tom, Tom, of Islington
Married a wife on Sunday,
Brought her home on Monday,
Hired a house on Tuesday,
Fed her well on Wednesday,
Sick was she on Thursday,
Dead was she on Friday,
Sad was Tom on Saturday
To bury his wife on Sunday.

## Taffy Was a Welshman

TAFFY was a Welshman, Taffy was a thief,
Taffy came to my house and stole a leg of beef.
I went to Taffy's house, Taffy wasn't in,
So I jumped upon his favourite hat and poked it with a pin.

Taffy was a Welshman, Taffy was a sham,
Taffy came to my house and stole a leg of lamb.
I went to Taffy's house and Taffy was away,
So I filled his socks with sawdust and stuffed his shoes
    with clay.

Taffy was a Welshman, Taffy was a cheat,
Taffy came to my house and stole a piece of meat.
I went to Taffy's house, Taffy was not there,
So I put his coat and trousers to roast before the fire.

The origins of this rhyme are believed to lie in Welsh mythology, in which Taffy may be equated with Amaethon, son of Don, and the Celtic god of agriculture. The myth has it that Amaethon once stole a lapwing, a roebuck and a dog from Arawan, the king of the otherworld. This theft led to a battle between the king and Amaethon, the latter aided by his siblings. One of them, Gwydion, used his magic powers and turned trees into brave warriors who then helped the Children of Don to victory.

The rhyme reflects the rivalry between the nations of England and Wales, historically pitted against each other. **Taffy,** as a corruption of 'Dafydd', Welsh for 'David' (Wales's patron saint), would have been the standard name for a Welshman; hence the rhyme was aimed at the Welsh in general and reflects how the English might have taught their children from the cradle never to trust their Celtic neighbours – that they were thieves, cheats and liars. Periodically, the Welsh – under English rule from 1284 – have rebelled against the English; this rhyme would appear to advocate harsh punishment for any Welshman stepping out of line. It's hardly surprising that when there was a referendum the Welsh decided to devolve from a government based in London.

# There Was a Crooked Man

THERE was a crooked man and he walked a crooked mile,
He found a crooked sixpence upon a crooked stile;
He bought a crooked cat, that caught a crooked mouse,
And they all lived together in their little crooked house.

'There Was a Crooked Man' has its roots in seventeenth-century English history and the career of General Sir Alexander Leslie (*c.*1580–1661), a Scottish soldier who also served with the Dutch and Swedish military. In the context of the rhyme, the word **crooked** is used not to suggest he was a frail, hunched old man, but to illustrate his perceived lack of loyalty and dishonesty. He was, in other words, bent.

During the Thirty Years' War (1618–48), when most of Europe was a battleground fought over by the Protestants and Catholics, Leslie distinguished himself fighting for the Dutch before transferring to the Swedish army, where he rose to the rank of colonel and was knighted by the Swedish king for his valour.

At the end of the conflict, Leslie returned to his native Scotland where he raised an army and seized Edinburgh Castle, without the loss of a single man, from the few remaining Scottish loyalists. He then turned south across the winding border with England (the **crooked mile**) and won a great victory for the Scots at the Battle of Newburn (1640), against the king's army, before taking control of

Newcastle, cutting off its valuable coal supply to London
and forcing Charles I into an agreement with Leslie's Scottish Covenanters – supporters of the National Covenant of

1638, denying the Divine Right of the king to be spiritual
leader of the Presbyterian Church – that led to the Treaty of
London.

As a result, in 1641, English King Charles I bestowed

upon Leslie the titles of Earl of Levin and Lord Balgonie after the Scot had changed his allegiance once again, this time from Scotland to England, amassing another small fortune in the process (**He found a crooked penny upon a crooked stile**). Charles also gave Leslie the position of Captain of Edinburgh Castle and made him a privy councillor, one of his closest and most trusted advisers, after Leslie had sworn a new allegiance to the troubled and beleaguered king.

But the new Earl of Leven once again broke his oath and, in 1644, raised an army and fought for the Solemn League and Covenant, a treaty binding both Scottish and English Parliaments together against the Royalist forces, and again marched south, to join Lord Fairfax in crushing Prince Rupert at the Battle of Marston Moor.

In 1646, King Charles, pursued by Oliver Cromwell's Parliamentarian forces, eventually surrendered to the Scots, after the Siege of Oxford, with whom he felt he would be safe and could hatch a deal with his new Earl of Leven. But Leven wasted no time in turning the king back over to the English, leading to Charles's eventual execution. After which the alliance between the previously warring Scots and the English held firm for a while (**They all lived together in their crooked little house**).

# There Was a Little Girl

THERE was a little girl
Who had a little curl
Right in the middle of her forehead.
When she was good,
She was very, very good,
But when she was bad she was horrid.

This popular nursery rhyme is unusual in having not just a famous author but also one who refused to be associated with it. Best known for his poem *The Song of Hiawatha*, Henry Wadsworth Longfellow (1807–82) was regarded in his day as the American Tennyson. Such was his fame and distinguished reputation that Longfellow always denied composing the childish verses. Once questioned by his friends on the subject, he angrily declared: 'When I recall my juvenile poems and prose sketches I wish they were entirely forgotten about. However, they cling to one's skirt with a terrible grasp.'

Eventually he admitted to having made up the rhyme when his young daughter petulantly refused to have her hair brushed. The poet's second son, Ernest, later recalled: 'It was whilst he was walking up and down with Edith, then a baby, in his arms that my father composed and sang to her the well-known lines. Many people think it is a Mother Goose rhyme, but this is the true origin and history.'

Ironically enough, this is now probably the best-known of all his poems.

# There Was a Little Guinea Pig

THERE was a little guinea pig,
Who being little was not big;
He always walked upon his feet,
And never fasted when he eat.

When from a place he ran away,
He never at the place did stay;
And while he ran, as I am told,
He ne'er stood still for young or old.

He often squeaked and sometimes violent,
And when he squeaked he ne'er was silent;
Though ne'er instructed by a cat,
He knew a mouse was not a rat.

One day, as I am certified,
He took a whim and fairly died;
And as I'm told by men of sense
He never has been living since.

Originating in South America, guinea pigs have been domesticated for over a thousand years (although they are still a favourite snack in Peru). They first came to Europe during the sixteenth century, following the discovery of the Americas, and legend has it that the first person in Britain to have one as a pet was Elizabeth I.

Unfortunately, this means that my favourite theory behind this rhyme now looks pretty far-fetched. According to this interpretation, the **guinea pig** is Richard III (1452–85). King Richard's royal emblem was a great white boar and to refer to him as a guinea pig was therefore a wholly intentional insult. The **cat** in verse three is supposedly William Catesby, Richard's Chancellor of the Exchequer and Speaker of the House of Commons (see also HEY DIDDLE DIDDLE). He was thought to be the most powerful man in England at the time and a huge influence on the king. The **rat** is Sir Richard Ratcliffe, a childhood friend and valued adviser of the king. The rhyme refers to the close relationship between the three men and the supposed influence the cat and the rat had over the king, but, as I said, this was over a century before guinea pigs came to England for the first time.

The lyrics probably have no hidden meaning but are just trying to be humorous, the whole purpose of the rhyme being its nonsensical yoking together of a string of tautological phrases – **being little was not big ... never fasted when he eat** – to make children laugh.

# There Was an Old Woman
# Who Lived in a Shoe

THERE was an old woman who lived in a shoe,
She had so many children she didn't know what to do;
So she gave them some broth without any bread,
And she whipped them all soundly and sent them to bed.

At first glance, this is simply another nonsense rhyme but there is, in fact, a story behind it, concerning George II (1683–1760; see also GEORGIE PORGIE). He was born in Hanover, Germany – the last British sovereign to have been born outside Britain – and English was therefore not his first language. His subjects found him rather hard to understand, and, not very impressed with him as a monarch, they nicknamed him the **old woman**. It was after all his wife, Queen Caroline, who was the real power behind the throne and made all the major decisions, as a contemporary verse sneers:

> You may strut, dapper George,
> But it will be in vain;
> We all know it is Queen Caroline
> Not you that reign.

This was underlined further by his having very little control over parliamentary policy during the early part of his reign as the government was firmly controlled at that time by Britain's first prime minister, Sir Robert Walpole (chosen by

Caroline). Hence the **children** in the rhyme are the members of Parliament that he had so little control over. The bursting of the South Sea Bubble of 1721 had left Britain impoverished and George II was perpetually struggling to save money to improve Britain's (and his own) financial situation (**she gave them some broth without any bread**), mainly so he could go to war again and prove by attacking other countries that he really was in control of his own. A **whip** is the MP whose job it is to ensure other members of their party are present to vote on a particular policy their faction feels strongly about, and the **bed** was the Houses of Parliament, which the king required his MPs to attend every day.

Another theory considers the **shoe** from the point of view of its associations with female fertility – hence the casting of a shoe after the bride, or attaching shoes to the car of the bridal couple in the hope that their union will be fruitful. George and Caroline were clearly not lacking in that department as they had eight children. Indeed, Caroline – and a number of other prominent women with large families – has been identified with the **old woman** (**She had so many children she didn't know what to do**).

# Three Acres of Land

MY father left me three acres of land,
Sing ivy, sing ivy;
My father left me three acres of land,
Sing holly, go whistle and ivy.

I ploughed it with the ram's horn,
Sing ivy, sing ivy;
And sowed it all over with one peppercorn,
Sing holly, go whistle and ivy.

I harrowed it with the bramble bush,
Sing ivy, sing ivy;
And reaped it with my little penknife,
Sing holly, go whistle and ivy.

I got the mice to carry it to the barn,
Sing ivy, sing ivy;
And threshed it with a goose's quill,
Sing holly, go whistle and ivy.

I got the puss to carry it to the mill,
Sing ivy, sing ivy;
The miller he swore he would have her paw
And the cat she swore she would scratch his face,
Sing holly, go whistle and ivy.

This nonsense rhyme, which shows step by ridiculous step how not to run a farm, sheds an interesting light on how things were actually done in the past. An acre of land was originally thought to be the area of farmland that could be ploughed by an ox in half a day. From the seventeenth century, this was standardized to 4,840 square yards, or about the size of a modern football pitch. Thus, however you measure it, three acres represents a reasonably large plot of land.

Ploughing that amount of land would have needed oxen or horses and a proper plough. The crop to be planted – **pepper** – was very valuable but one that would never grow in Britain's cold climate. Pepper was a highly prized spice, first used by the Egyptians as long ago as 2000 BC. Thanks to their natural longevity (they could last for many years) and their shortage of supply, peppercorns were once valued as highly as gold and were often used as trading currency. In the Middle Ages, explorers such as Christopher Columbus and Marco Polo set off on their adventures in the hope of finding new sources of pepper and other valuable spices.

Rather than weeding the fields, the song's hero uses the brambles as an impossible rake (**I harrowed the field with a bramble bush**); rather than a scythe he uses a **penknife**; he gets **mice** and **cats** to carry the crops for him, and tries to thresh it with a feather (**a goose's quill**). In short, it's a farmer's sly song about what might happen if a landowner gifted some of the land to his own offspring (**My father left** me three acres of land). With no farming know-how, they wouldn't have a clue how to go about things.

## Three Blind Mice

> THREE blind mice, three blind mice,
> See how they run, see how they run;
> They all ran after the farmer's wife,
> Who cut off their tails with a carving knife;
> Did you ever see such a thing in your life,
> As three blind mice?

The origin of the words to 'Three Blind Mice' lies with the English queen Mary I (1516–58), known as Bloody Mary because she was prepared to do anything – however violent – to make sure England became Catholic again. Mary was the only child of Henry VIII and his first wife, the Spanish princess Catherine of Aragon (see I HAD A LITTLE NUT TREE). Henry had initially doted upon Mary and boasted about her publicly, even breaking royal protocol by giving her the title of Princess of Wales, a prerogative usually reserved for the male firstborn, but all this changed when Catherine failed to produce a male heir, leading to events that marked a major watershed in English history.

When Henry attempted to dissolve his marriage to Mary's mother, on the grounds Catherine had previously been briefly married, as a sixteen-year-old, to his elder brother Arthur, who then died only a few days later. In his despera-

tion for a divorce and a male heir with another wife, Henry
tried to show God was on his side by citing passages from
the Bible: 'If a man shall take his brother's wife, it is an
unclean thing; he hath uncovered his brother's nakedness
and they shall remain childless' (Leviticus 20:21). When
Pope Clement VII refused his request, Henry broke English

links with the Catholic Church and declared himself head of
the newly reformed Church of England. He then promptly
married Anne Boleyn, who was to prove no more successful
at producing a male heir than her predecessor. As a result of
the divorce, Catherine lost the title of queen and Mary was
declared illegitimate, demoted from 'princess' to 'lady' and
lost her position at court – earning the nickname, according
to some, of the **Farmer's Wife**, although this is more likely
to be a reference to the vast estates she would own as wife

of King Philip of Spain (see FLOUR OF ENGLAND). For Thomas Cranmer, the man who eventually sanctioned Henry's second marriage, there would be dire consequences.

Meanwhile Henry began confiscating land from the Catholics and dissolving the monasteries. During his brief reign, Henry's son Edward VI (1537–53) took things much further and started hunting down and executing Catholic priests. The three religious leaders supporting Edward during this time were the bishops Hugh Latimer and Nicholas Ridley and the ever-loyal Archbishop of Canterbury, Thomas Cranmer, architect of Henry VIII's English Reformation. Openly Catholic, Mary was seen as a real danger to newly Protestant England, and the policies set in motion by these three were openly unfriendly: in effect, **They all ran after the farmer's wife.**

Unluckily for them, Edward only lasted six years. When Mary I finally ascended the throne in 1553, the bitter queen immediately set about restoring the Catholic faith as the religion of England and the real bloodletting began. Over eight hundred wealthy Protestants fled the country and nearly three hundred were burned at the stake in what became known as the Marian Persecutions (see MARY, MARY, QUITE CONTRARY). The most high-profile of these victims, later remembered as the 'Oxford Martyrs', were Latimer, Ridley and Cranmer, who were tortured, some stories say blinded, and then burned at the stake in central Oxford in front of hundreds of shocked spectators (she **cut off their tails with a carving knife; / Did you ever see such a thing in your life**).

Another, less convincing theory is that three blind commoners, Joan Waste, John Aprice and an unspecified third, defied Queen Mary's ban on reading the Bible in English and between them paid for a copy to have it read to them in public, as a result of which they were also burned at the stake.

The first written version of 'Three Blind Mice' was published between 1609 and 1611 by Thomas Ravenscroft (1582–1635), whose booklets *Pammelia* (1609), *Deutero-melia* (1609) and *Melismata* (1611) brought together a collection of street songs, ballads, poems and children's songs that included 'Three Blind Mice', although with slightly different lyrics to the ones we know so well today:

> Three Blinde Mice,
> Three Blinde Mice,
> Dame Iulian,
> Dame Iulian,
> The Miller and his merry olde Wife,
> Shee scrapte her tripe licke thou the knife,
> The Three Blinde Mice.

Publishing the poem only fifty years after Queen Mary's Persecutions, Ravenscroft, a noted scholar, composer and musician, could have been recording a well-known rhyme of its day or, as some believe, may even have composed it himself. While authorship of the rhyme is a matter of dispute, what is generally accepted is that 'Three Blind Mice' refers to the brutal slaying of the three bishops ('she scraped off the entrails and licked the knife', to translate line 6) opposed to Queen Mary's religious reforms, one of whom had made the mistake of dissolving Mary's mother's marriage to King Henry VIII and reducing her status from princess to commoner. And it meant that from the moment Mary became queen, Thomas Cranmer must have known his days were numbered.

# Tom, Tom, the Piper's Son

TOM, Tom, the piper's son,
He learned to play when he was young,
But the only tune that he could play
Was 'Over the hills and far away'.
Over the hills and a great way off,
The wind shall blow my top-knot off.

Tom with his pipe did play with skill,
And those who heard him couldn't keep still;
Whenever they heard him they would dance,
Even the sheep would after him prance.

According to one theory, 'Tom, Tom, the Piper's Son' evolved from an old legend about the son of a Scottish bagpiper who would play his pipes while out on the hills looking after his flock of sheep. But Tom only knew one tune (**the only tune that he could play**), which he played over and over again. Even so, the tree spirits would emerge and dance to this tune whenever Tom played (**Whenever they heard him they would dance**). The Celts believed that trees possessed magical and mystical powers, and it is from this belief that a wand acquires its magic and the modern tree huggers get their empathy with nature.

So it makes me feel very cynical to have to point out, however, that the rhyme itself can't be all that old as it contains a reference to 'Over the Hills and Far Away', a well-known song from the early eighteenth century, of which there is a version in George Farquhar's *The Recruiting Officer* (1706) and John Gay's *The Beggar's Opera* (1728). But the refrain **Over the hills and far away** appears in many other poems and songs, suggesting a traditional origin, and **Tom** was a traditional name for pipers.

Another, equally familiar, version of the rhyme goes:

> Tom, Tom, the piper's son,
> Stole a pig and away did run.
> The pig was eat
> And Tom was beat,
> And Tom went howling down the street.

This version would seem to belong to that category of rhymes with a moral (see also LITTLE BO PEEP and MARY HAD A LITTLE LAMB), here pointing out to children the punishment that may befall them if they try to steal – a beating severe enough to make them cry (**Tom went howling down the street**). The **pig** in question would have been a sweetmeat one sold by a street hawker, so no animals were harmed in the making of this rhyme, its message was that children had to learn that stealing is stealing, whatever the value of the object stolen.

## Turn Again, Whittington

TURN again, Whittington, thou worthy citizen,
Turn again, Whittington, Lord Mayor of London.
Make your fortune, find a good wife,
You will know happiness all through your life.
Turn again, Whittington, thou worthy citizen,
Turn again, Whittington, thrice Mayor of London.

Thanks to this rhyme – sung as a round (see LONDON'S BURNING) – and his representation in pantomime in the manner of a fairy-tale character such as Cinderella or Aladdin, one might be forgiven for thinking that Dick Whittington is fictional, but he was a real person.

Born in the village of Pauntley in Gloucestershire around 1354, Richard Whittington went to London as a boy, after supposedly being told the streets there were 'paved with gold', to learn the trade of a mercer (trader in textiles). He worked hard and soon became successful, importing exotic new material such as velvet and silk and exporting English wool in return (see BAA, BAA, BLACK SHEEP). By 1397, he was making such a fortune that he started lending vast sums of money to the king, Richard II. In return, the king granted him the prestigious position of Lord Mayor of London. Richard Whittington worked just as hard at

making a success of his new role and proved to be so popular that he retained the honour for an unheard-of second
year.

But when King Richard was deposed, in 1399, Whittington feared for his future and decided to return to

Gloucestershire and a comfortable retirement. It was on
his journey out of London, legend has it, that at High-
gate Hill he heard the peal of Bow Bell (see ORANGES
AND LEMONS), calling him back to the city: **Turn again,
Whittington**. The popular merchant duly returned and

prospered even further under Richard's successors, Henry IV and Henry V, supplying the court with valuable textiles and cloth. In 1406, Whittington became Lord Mayor of London for the third time (**thrice Mayor of London**) and again, for a final term in office in 1419, although the rhyme doesn't allude to that.

He never forgot his humble origins, however, and was fondly known by Londoners as Dick, rather than Richard, Whittington. During his lifetime, he donated most of his profits to the City of London, financing many improvements for the benefit of the common people, such as public drinking fountains, a ward at St Thomas's Hospital for unmarried mothers, and accommodation for the homeless. He also rebuilt the Guildhall, paid for basic drainage systems and sanitation in slum areas and built Greyfriars Library to help improve education in that area.

When he died, in 1423, he left £7,000 to the Company of Mercers (equivalent to around £5 million in modern terms), which funded construction of the Guildhall Library, repairs to St Bartholomew's Hospital and the building of further almshouses for the homeless. In death, Dick Whittington became something of a folk hero and his legend is sure to live on. The only unfortunate part is there appears to be no mention anywhere in records of his life of his faithful cat, made famous by its appearance in story and pantomime. Although the image of a cat is supposed to have been carved above the gates of Newgate Prison after his death and, some say, also painted on a carriage presented in Whittington's name in 1572 to the Guild of Merchants, there is no real evidence to substantiate either of these claims.

It is through the legend of Dick Whittington that the expression 'The streets are paved with gold' has passed into common usage to describe a town or city full of opportunity and well worth a visit for the aspiring young entrepreneur. The first record of any London play about the former Lord Mayor dates from around 1605 with a production entitled *The History of Richard Whittington, of his lowe byrth and his great fortune.* Later in the century, Samuel Pepys wrote in his diary in 1668: 'Then to Southwark fair, very dirty, but saw the puppet show of Whittington, which was pretty to see.' In 1814, Dick Whittington made his debut as a pantomime character, with one of the greatest clowns of all time, Joseph Grimaldi (1778–1837), playing the role of Dame Cecily Suet. Chiefly thanks to pantomime, London's most famous Lord Mayor still lives on today.

# Tweedledum and Tweedledee

TWEEDLEDUM and Tweedledee
Agreed to have a battle;
For Tweedledum said Tweedledee
Had spoiled his nice new rattle.

Just then flew down a monstrous crow,
As black as a tar-barrel;
Which frightened both the heroes so,
They quite forgot their battle.

Tweedledum and Tweedledee found fame as fictional characters in Lewis Carroll's *Through the Looking-Glass, and What Alice Found There*, published in 1871. Carroll describes the two as a pair of tubby brothers whom Alice comes across on her travels and who put her in mind of 'the old song', which the brothers later act out. Carroll's illustrator, John Tenniel (see also HUMPTY DUMPTY and THE QUEEN OF HEARTS), depicted the 'fat little men' as identical twins, 'like a couple of great schoolboys', completely indistinguishable from each other. And that is why the expression **Tweedledum and Tweedledee** is used to this day to describe any two persons or objects that are so alike they cannot be identified individually.

But he didn't invent them. They were figures from a nursery rhyme Carroll would have heard as a child. The original Tweedledum and Tweedledee made their first appearance at least a century earlier, in a poem published in 1725 making fun of two feuding composers, Giovanni Battista Bononcini (1670–1747) and George Frideric Handel (1685–1759).

Handel and Bononcini had a long history. In Berlin in 1696, the young Handel was recognized as a child prodigy. At the royal court he met an established Italian composer, Bononcini. The older composer was instantly jealous of the young newcomer and attempted to injure his reputation by composing a particularly testing piece for the harpsichord and then asking him to play it at sight. When Handel executed it without a mistake, the schemer was foiled by his own device and duly hated the younger man all the more for it.

Twenty-four years later, in London, a number of noblemen formed themselves into a company for the purpose of reviving Italian opera in England. The king himself, George I, subscribed £1,000, and allowed the society to take the name of the Royal Academy of Music. Handel was appointed Director of Music.

Bononcini and Attilio Ariosti were attracted to London by this new venture, and stage two of the rivalry followed. The composition of a new opera, *Muzio Scevola*, was divided between the three composers. Attilio was to put the first act to music, Bononcini the second, and Handel the third, but a dispute developed between the latter two. Amused by this bout of semiquavers at ten paces, the poet John Byrom wrote:

> Some say, compar'd to Bononcini,
> That Mynheer Handel's but a Ninny;
> Others aver, that he to Handel
> Is scarcely fit to hold a Candle:
> Strange all this difference should be
> 'Twixt Tweedle-dum and Tweedle-dee!

Clearly Byrom is suggesting a small **dum** here and a tiny **dee** there are the only real discernible differences in the two composing styles – in which **Tweedle-dum** and **Tweedle-dee** sound like a mocking representation of their music – or, at least, that is what they were arguing over. Handel was extremely put out by this – he didn't want to be identified as part of a matching pair with his nemesis – and so, when the opportunity to get rid of Bononcini arose, he grabbed it ...

This all came courtesy of another composer and former friend of Handel, Maurice Greene (1676–1755). A gifted composer in his own right, Greene had once been close to Handel but they had fallen out when the latter found Greene was also friends with Bononcini. As a result, Greene's friendship with Bononcini became even closer; indeed, in 1728 Bononcini fashioned the madrigal 'In Una Siepe Ombrosa' ('In a Shady Hedge'), attributing the piece to his new friend in an attempt to help raise his profile. Unfortunately, another composer, Antonio Lotti, then complained he had written the music thirty years earlier and was able to produce eight separate witnesses who were prepared to confirm they had heard Lotti play the piece in rehearsal. Bononcini was thrown out of the Academy in disgrace, Handel pouring scorn on him in public at every opportunity, and eventually driven from London. Despite

never having signed the work, or so much as even claiming authorship, Bononcini's reputation hung in tatters and he's now barely remembered. He died alone in 1747 somewhere near Vienna.

# Twinkle, Twinkle, Little Star

TWINKLE, twinkle, little star,
How I wonder what you are;
Up above the world so high,
Like a diamond in the sky.
Twinkle, twinkle, little star,
How I wonder what you are.

This famous rhyme is actually a shorter version of a poem called 'The Star', written in 1806 by Jane Taylor (1783–1824). Only twenty-three years old when she composed it, Taylor wrote many collections with her sister Mary, notably *Original Poems for Infant Minds* (1804) and *Hymns for Infant Minds* (1808).

However, the well-known melody accompanying the words is French in origin, based on a song called '*Ah! vous dirai-je, Maman*' ('Ah! Let me tell you, Mama') and first published in 1761. The message of the song is somewhat different to 'Twinkle, Twinkle'. For those of us who cannot speak French, it can be roughly translated as:

Ah! Let me tell you, Mama,
What causes my torment.
Papa wants me to reason
Like a grown-up;
But me, I say that sweets have
Greater value than reason.

It is often claimed that Wolfgang Amadeus Mozart (1756–91) composed the tune, but he was only six years old in 1761 when the French folksong was first published. It's much more likely that he borrowed the folk tune as a motif for the piano variations that he wrote as a seventeen-year-old. As the third famous rhyme to have come from Colchester (see HUMPTY DUMPTY and OLD KING COLE), a plaque is now fixed to the wall of the Taylors' house in the old Dutch quarter of the city in honour of the author of the English poem.

The original version of 'The Star' had five verses of four lines each:

> Twinkle, twinkle, little star,
> How I wonder what you are;
> Up above the world so high
> Like a diamond in the sky.
>
> When the blazing sun is gone,
> When he no longer shines upon,
> Then you show your little light,
> Twinkle, twinkle, all the night.
>
> Then the traveller in the dark
> Thanks you for your tiny spark;
> He could not see the way to go
> If you did not twinkle so.

In the dark blue sky you keep
And often through my curtains peep,
For you never shut your eye
Till the sun is in the sky.

As your bright and tiny spark
Lights the traveller in the dark,
Though I know not what you are,
Twinkle, twinkle, little star.

Personally, I've always preferred Lewis Carroll's nonsense parody of this, sung by the Mad Hatter in *Alice's Adventures in Wonderland* (1865):

Twinkle, twinkle, little bat,
How I wonder what you're at!
Up above the world you fly,
Like a tea-tray in the sky.

# Wee Willie Winkie

WEE Willie Winkie runs through the town,
Upstairs and downstairs in his nightgown,
Tapping at the window and crying through the lock:
Are all the children in their beds, it's past eight o'clock!

Some have suggested this rhyme is about William of Orange, pointing to the unpopular rules and curfews that he imposed upon England after he had replaced James II

as king in 1689. It is certainly true that William's Act of
Toleration of the same year, guaranteeing religious freedom, actually extended only to Protestant non-conformists
whereas Roman Catholics were shown no tolerance at all
but kept under close scrutiny.

However, that's pretty unlikely to be the origin of this
rhyme, considering that its first publication date was 1841 –
centuries after the reign of William of Orange. In fact the
author of the poem was himself called William. William
Miller (1810–72) was a Scottish poet; the version we know
is a translation from the Scots and there are nineteen more
verses. Here are just four (also in translation) to show how
the poem develops:

> 'Hey, Willie Winkie, are you coming in?
> The cat is singing purring sounds to the sleeping hen,
> The dog's spread out on the floor, and doesn't give a cheep,
> But here's a wakeful little boy who will not fall asleep!'
>
> Anything but sleep, you rogue! glowering like the moon,
> Rattling in an iron jug with an iron spoon,
> Rumbling, tumbling round about, crowing like a cock,
> Shrieking like I don't know what, waking sleeping folk.
>
> 'Hey, Willie Winkie – the child's in a creel!
> Wriggling from everyone's knee like an eel,
> Tugging at the cat's ear, and confusing all her thrums
> Hey, Willie Winkie – see, there he comes!'

Weary is the mother who has a dusty child,
A small short little child, who can't run on his own,
Who always has a battle with sleep before he'll close an eye
But a kiss from his rosy lips gives strength anew to me.

So, far from being a Dutch king imposing a curfew on the nation, Wee Willie is actually a magical creature, like the Sandman, that brings sleep to children. In his poem, which would have been recited to children at bedtime (and perhaps that's why there are so many tedious extra verses – to bore them to sleep), William Miller created a popular figure in much the same way as the anonymous contemporary poem 'A Visit From St Nicholas' (published in 1823 and better known as ''Twas the Night Before Christmas') had pinned down Father Christmas properly for the first time.

## What Are Little Boys Made Of?

WHAT are little boys made of?
What are little boys made of?
Slugs and snails and puppy dogs' tails,
That's what little boys are made of.

What are little girls made of?
What are little girls made of?
Sugar and spice and all things nice,
That's what li' le girls are made of.

This well-known rhyme is part of a much longer work credited to the English poet Robert Southey (1774–1843) and called 'What All the World Is Made Of', written around 1820.

After a revolutionary youth – at one stage, he and fellow poet Samuel Taylor Coleridge planned to set up a utopian community in America – Robert Southey became part of the establishment. Made Poet Laureate in 1813, he was very famous in his lifetime. His popular biography of Lord Nelson re-established a rather scandalous figure as one of England's great heroes. Southey took himself and his writing extremely seriously, so, like Longfellow (see THERE WAS A LITTLE GIRL), he would have been horrified to learn that his nonsensical jingle for children is now his best-known poem.

The remaining verses of the rhyme – the language updated from that of Southey's original poem – go like this:

> What are little babies made of?
> What are little babies made of?
> Nappies and crumbs and sucking their thumbs,
> That's what little babies are made of.

> What are young men made of?
> What are young men made of?
> Sighs and leers and crocodile tears,
> That's what young men are made of.

What are young women made of?
What are young women made of?
Rings and jings and other fine things,
That's what young women are made of.

What are our sailors made of?
What are our sailors made of?
Pitch and tar, pig-tail and scar,
That's what our sailors are made of.

What are our soldiers made of?
What are our soldiers made of?
Pipeclay and drill, the foeman to kill,
That's what our soldiers are made of.

What are our nurses made of?
What are our nurses made of?
Bushes and thorns and old cow's horns,
That's what our nurses are made of.

What are our fathers made of?
What are our fathers made of?
Pipes and smoke and collars that choke,
That's what our fathers are made of.

What are our mothers made of?
What are our mothers made of?
Ribbons and laces and sweet pretty faces,
That's what our mothers are made of.

What are old men made of?
What are old men made of?
Slippers that flop and a bald-headed top,
That's what old men are made of.

What are old women made of?
What are old women made of ?
Reels, and jeels and old spinning wheels,
That's what old women are made of.

What is all the world made of?
What is all the world made of?
Fighting a spot and loving a lot,
That's what all the world's made of.

# Who Killed Cock Robin?

WHO killed Cock Robin?
I, said the Sparrow,
With my bow and arrow,
I killed Cock Robin.

Who saw him die?
I, said the Fly,
With my little eye,
I saw him die.

Who caught his blood?
I, said the Fish,
With my little dish,
I caught his blood.

Who will make the shroud?
I, said the Beetle,
With my thread and needle,
I'll make the shroud.

Who will dig his grave?
I, said the Owl,
With my pick and shovel,
I will dig his grave.

Who will be the parson?
I, said the Rook,
With my little book,
I shall be the parson.

Who will be the clerk?
I, said the Lark,
If it is not in the dark,
I will be the clerk.

Who will carry the link?
I, said the Linnet,
I will fetch it in a minute,
I'll carry the link.

Who will be chief mourner?
I, said the Dove,
I mourn for my love,
I will be chief mourner.

Who will carry the coffin?
I, said the Kite,
If it's not through the night,
I will carry the coffin.

Who will bear the pall?
We, said the Wren,
Both the cock and the hen,
We'll bear the pall.

Who will sing a psalm?
I, said the Thrush
As she sat on a bush,
I will sing a psalm.

Who will toll the bell?
I, said the Bull,
Because I can pull,
I will toll the bell.

All the birds of the air
Fell a-sighing and a-sobbing
When they heard the bell toll
For poor Cock Robin.

A tragic tale told in timeless language, 'Who Killed Cock Robin?' is in some ways more akin to a folksong than a nursery rhyme. Like many rhymes, however, it has a repetitive format that creates a cumulative effect (see FOR WANT OF A NAIL and THIS IS THE HOUSE THAT JACK BUILT), as the various birds are listed, along with their rhyming actions. But is the rhyme more than just a glorified avian roll-call?

As so often with traditional songs and rhymes, various theories about this one's origins abound but with little evidence to back them up. The most popular of these suggests that the song is about the death of the folk hero Robin Hood, or 'Cocky Robin', and that all the birds and animals of Sherwood Forest are mourning him. However, the only link between the famous outlaw and the rhyme lies in the name **Robin** and in the connection with archery; the stories are otherwise very different. According to the legend, Robin Hood dies at the hands of a prioress, his cousin, who bleeds him to death. By the time Little John, his right-hand man, gets to him, he's already dying. With one final burst of strength, he shoots an arrow out of the tower window to the spot where he wishes to be buried, and then he promptly passes away.

Another theory concerns the story of William Rufus, son of William the Conqueror and king of England from 1087 to 1100, who was mysteriously shot with an arrow while hunting in the New Forest. The Rufus Stone, erected in 1865, marks the spot where he was supposedly killed, but there's little evidence of any connection between his death and the nursery rhyme.

The rhyme was first published in 1744, and it has been argued that it is actually a political poem about the downfall of Robert Walpole's government two years earlier. However, its language and content suggest it is a lot older than that.

But the most likely interpretation harks back to medieval folk beliefs about the robin. Traditionally the bird got its red breast from trying to wipe the blood away from the face of Jesus on the cross. Hence from the Middle Ages onwards, the robin was seen as a symbol of Christ. The poem is also strikingly ritualistic. The important events are the death and funeral of Cock Robin – there is no blame or retribution. It was once commonly believed (indeed, Thomas Hardy wrote a poem about it – 'The Oxen') that all farmyard animals knelt at midnight on Christmas Eve to celebrate Christ's birth. Echoing this, the rhyme shows animals mourning his death on Good Friday.

# TRADITIONAL
# SONGS AND
# ANTHEMS

# Amazing Grace

AMAZING grace, how sweet the sound
That saved a wretch like me!
I once was lost, but now I'm found,
Was blind, but now I see.

'Twas grace that taught my heart to fear,
And grace my fear relieved;
How precious did that grace appear,
The hour I first believed!

Through many dangers, toils and snares,
I have already come;
'Tis grace that brought me safe thus far,
And grace will lead me home.

The Lord has promised good to me,
His Word my hope secures;
He will my shield and portion be,
As long as life endures.

Yes, when this heart and flesh shall fail,
And mortal life shall cease,
I shall possess, within the veil,
A life of health and peace.

> The world shall soon dissolve like snow,
> The sun forbear to shine;
> But God, who called me here below,
> Shall be forever mine.

'Amazing Grace' is one of the most popular and easily recognizable Christian hymns, but its strong connections with slavery are not so well known. And nor is the name of the man who wrote the lyrics.

John Newton was born in London on 24 July 1725, the son of a ship master. He first joined his father at sea in 1736, aged only eleven, his father's plan being for the youngster to become a slave master on a plantation in the West Indies in due course. But this, like all best-laid plans, went astray a few years later when Newton was seized by a press gang and forced aboard a ship, the HMS *Harwich*, bound for Africa. After attempting to escape, the nineteen-year-old was clamped in irons, flogged in front of the 350-man crew and placed on a slave ship, where he was treated very harshly for the next three years. Eventually Newton was rescued by a friend of his father, who had asked him to 'keep an eye out' for his missing son. On the journey back to England aboard another slave ship, the *Greyhound*, they encountered a severe storm that nearly wrecked the vessel. During the night, as the boat's hull filled with water, Newton prayed for salvation and the storm, which had raged for many days, finally subsided, so that the ship and its crew were saved. It was 10 March 1748, a date Newton was to celebrate for the rest of his days.

The incident changed Newton's life, convincing him of God's grace and turning him to Christianity (**I once was lost, but now am found**), and from then onwards he avoided

drinking, gambling and any form of profanity. It also changed his attitude towards the brutal slave trade; still sailing along the slave routes, he did not challenge slave trafficking – or not until many years later – but ensured that his human cargo was well treated during the voyage. When

illness forced him to retire from the sea in 1754, he followed
his spiritual leanings and became curator of Olney Church
in Buckinghamshire. In 1772, Newton wrote 'Amazing
Grace' about his near-death experience aboard the *Greyhound* and his subsequent conversion. The following
year, he became rector of St Mary Woolchurch in London
where, among his new congregation, he met William
Wilberforce who, under the rector's influence, was to
become the driving force and leader of the movement to
abolish slavery.

# God Save the Queen

GOD save our gracious Queen,
Long live our noble Queen,
God save the Queen!
Send her victorious,
Happy and glorious,
Long to reign over us;
God save the Queen!

Thy choicest gifts in store
On her be pleased to pour;
Long may she reign.
May she defend our laws,
And ever give us cause
To sing with heart and voice,
God save the Queen!

The expression 'God save the king' first appeared in print in the King James Bible in 1611 but is thought to have been a catchphrase of the Royal Navy as early as 1545. In 1739, the composer Thomas Augustine Arne (1710–78), who also

created 'Rule Britannia', wrote an early version of the words and set them to music to be performed at a dinner in 1740 in London to celebrate the first victory in the War of Jenkins' Ear.

Both 'Rule Britannia' and 'God Save the King' were intended to encourage patriotic support for George II at a troubled time in English history. The War of Jenkins' Ear with Spain – sparked off by one Robert Jenkins, the captain of a smuggling vessel whose ear was supposedly severed in a tussle with the Spanish coastguard – was just about to escalate into the War of the Austrian Succession. Meanwhile, back at home, there was the Second Jacobite Rebellion to contend with – one of two uprisings aimed at restoring Stuart kings to the British throne; an army led by the Young Pretender, 25-year-old Bonnie Prince Charlie, attacked and initially defeated the king's men at the Battle of Prestonpans (see also ELSIE MARLEY, THE LION AND THE UNICORN and THE SKYE BOAT SONG).

The song first appeared in print on 15 October 1745, when it was published in *The Gentlemen's Magazine*, and billed as 'God save our lord the king: A new song set for two voices'. The current official version has been in use since 1919 courtesy of King George V, who, due to the number of times he had heard it played, considered himself to be 'something of an expert', and in 1933 a proclamation was issued, setting out the melody, tempo and orchestration that has been in use ever since.

# Good King Wenceslas

GOOD King Wenceslas looked out, on the Feast of Stephen,
When the snow lay round about, deep and crisp and even;
Brightly shone the moon that night, though the frost was cruel,
When a poor man came in sight, gathering winter fuel.

'Hither, page, and stand by me, if thou know'st it, telling,
Yonder peasant, who is he? Where and what his dwelling?'
'Sire, he lives a good league hence, underneath the mountain;
Right against the forest fence, by Saint Agnes' fountain.'

'Bring me flesh, and bring me wine, bring me pine logs hither;
Thou and I will see him dine, when we bear them thither.'
Page and monarch, forth they went, forth they went together,
Through the rude wind's wild lament and the bitter weather.

'Sire, the night is darker now, and the wind blows stronger;
Fails my heart, I know not how; I can go no longer.'
'Mark my footsteps, my good page, tread thou in them boldly;
Thou shalt find the winter's rage freeze thy blood less coldly.'

In his master's steps he trod, where the snow lay dinted;
Heat was in the very sod which the saint had printed.
Therefore, Christian men, be sure, wealth or rank possessing,
Ye who now will bless the poor, shall yourselves find
    blessing.

This popular Christmas carol was written by John Mason Neale (1819–66), warden of Sackville College in Sussex. He was inspired by the legend of Wenceslas I, Duke of Bohemia (907–35) – patron saint of the Czech Republic. Wenceslas was a Christian and the carol stresses his virtue and religious humility, but these are more the stuff of legend than strictly accurate. He was canonized less for leading an exemplary life than for the manner of his death – murdered at the age of twenty-eight in a plot orchestrated by his younger brother – and because of the various miracles that were supposed to have taken place shortly after he died.

Czech legend has it that (like King Arthur) he sleeps with a huge army of knights, in the Blaník Mountain, and will awake to defend the nation should it ever be in direst need. There is also a tradition in Prague which states that when the Motherland is in its darkest hour and close to ruin, the equestrian statue of King Wenceslas in Wenceslas Square will come to life and wake the army slumbering beneath the mountain. Although, after sleeping through the whole of the Second World War and the Russian invasion of 1968, this army is clearly quite hard to rouse.

# The Hokey Cokey

YOU put your right hand in,
You put your right hand out,
You put your right hand in
And you shake it all about.

You do the Hokey Cokey
And you turn around;
That's what it's all about.

You put your left hand in,
You put your left hand out,
You put your left hand in
And you shake it all about.

You do the Hokey Cokey
And you turn around;
That's what it's all about.

You put your right leg in,
You put your right leg out,
You put your right leg in
And you shake it all about.

You do the Hokey Cokey
And you turn around;
That's what it's all about.

> You put your left leg in,
> You put your left leg out,
> You put your left leg in
> And you shake it all about.
>
> You do the Hokey Cokey
> And you turn around;
> That's what it's all about.

A popular party song the world over, this always reminds me of the story of the poor chap who wrote it and the day they buried him. Apparently, after preparing his body at the funeral parlour, they tried to lift him into a coffin. But as soon as they put his left leg in everything went wrong for them.

The general belief is that Charles Macak, Tafit Baker and Larry LaPrise wrote the American version of the song, 'The Hokey Pokey', in 1949 to entertain skiers at the Sun Valley resort in Idaho, USA. But the song is older than that. For a start, 'The Hokey Cokey' was a well-known British wartime music-hall song, first credited to Jimmy Kennedy, the composer of other enduring hits such as 'Teddy Bears' Picnic'. British bandleader Gerry Hoey also claimed authorship in 1940 of a similar tune, 'The Hoey Oka'.

The origins of the song go back much further than that, however. Some argue that **Hokey Cokey** is a corruption of the '*hocus pocus*' beloved of magicians, an expression that derives, in turn, from the words of the Catholic Mass, *hoc corpus meum*, 'this is my body', indicating the conversion of the Communion 'bread' into the body of Christ. The Puritans, against anything that could be construed as idolatrous (see RIDE A COCK HORSE TO BANBURY CROSS), mocked the accompanying words as a kind of magical incantation.

The dance that goes with the song – in which the participants all dance in a ring, putting the relevant limb in and out, and then shaking it about – goes back a fair way too. Similar dances and songs were recorded in Robert Chambers's *Popular Rhymes of Scotland* (1826), and other versions have been traced to seventeenth-century minstrels. 'The Hokey Cokey' would appear to parody the religious rituals of the Shakers (so named for their jerky movements while engaged in worship), who both danced and sang during their services. But the earliest accurate record, so far, of the song we all know and love is from an account, dated 1857, of two sisters from Canterbury in England, on a trip to Bridgewater, New Hampshire. During their visit they taught the locals a song that went something like this:

> I put my right hand in,
> I put my right hand out,
> I give my hand a shake, shake, shake,
> And turn myself about.

Apparently the performance of the song – called 'Right Elbow In' and several verses long – was accompanied by 'appropriate gestures' and danced with a slow, rhythmic motion. Whether or not an earlier reference will be found, it seems that the origins of 'The Hokey Cokey' do not lie in America, as currently claimed; the song was merely exported there.

# I Saw Three Ships

I SAW three ships come sailing in,
On Christmas day, on Christmas day;
I saw three ships come sailing in,
On Christmas day in the morning.

And what was in those ships all three,
On Christmas day, on Christmas day?
And what was in those ships all three,
On Christmas day in the morning?

Our Saviour Christ and His lady,
On Christmas day, on Christmas day;
Our Saviour Christ and His lady,
On Christmas day in the morning.

Pray whither sailed those ships all three,
On Christmas day, on Christmas day?
Pray whither sailed those ships all three,
On Christmas day in the morning?

Oh, they sailed into Bethlehem,
On Christmas day, on Christmas day;
Oh, they sailed into Bethlehem,
On Christmas day in the morning.

And all the souls on Earth shall sing,
On Christmas day, on Christmas day;
And all the souls on Earth shall sing,
On Christmas day in the morning.

Then let us all rejoice amen,
On Christmas day, on Christmas day;
Then let us all rejoice amen,
On Christmas day in the morning.

Pedants among you may well be complaining that Bethlehem is nowhere near the sea. This very old song, sung as a Christmas carol, is believed to derive from a twelfth-century story about three ships bringing the relics of the Wise Men to Cologne in Germany. Hence in the song the **three ships** represent the three Wise Men journeying across the world to see the infant Jesus, while the ships' passengers are members of the Holy Family. Meanwhile the masts of the three ships – in illustrations of the carol – provide a less than cheery visual echo of the three crosses on Calvary, recalling the death as well as the birth of Jesus (see also WHO KILLED COCK ROBIN?).

Further speculation about the symbolism found within the carol has suggested that the ships are indirect references

to the Holy Trinity or to I Corinthians 13:13 (King James
Bible): 'And now abideth faith, hope, charity, these three;
but the greatest of these is charity.'

A wilder theory associates the rhyme with Christopher
Columbus – whose expedition to the New World consisted
of three small sailing ships, the *Niña*, the *Pinta* and the
*Santa María* – on his way to discover the Americas, the
enterprise backed by **his lady**, Queen Isabella of Spain.
There is no evidence to connect Columbus's voyage with
the nursery rhyme, but, as usual, that hasn't stopped some
people from perpetuating the myth.

Whatever the intentions of the song's lyricist, 'I Saw
Three Ships' had been a popular carol long before its first
publication in 1666. Sir Cecil Sharp, a collector of British
folksongs and legends, which he gathered together in his
work *The Bishoprick Garland* (1834), discovered several
versions of the song that go back many centuries.

# Jerusalem

AND did those feet in ancient time
Walk upon England's mountains green?
And was the holy Lamb of God
On England's pleasant pastures seen?

And did the Countenance Divine
Shine forth upon our clouded hills?
And was Jerusalem builded here
Among those dark satanic mills?

Bring me my bow of burning gold:
Bring me my arrows of desire:
Bring me my spear: O clouds, unfold!
Bring me my chariot of fire.

I will not cease from mental fight,
Nor shall my sword sleep in my hand:
Till we have built Jerusalem
In England's green and pleasant land.

Seen as the archetypal English song, many have called for 'Jerusalem' to become the new national anthem instead of GOD SAVE THE QUEEN. However, that was very far from the intentions of the poem's author, William Blake (1757–1827). Blake wrote this poem about the English poet John Milton (1608–74); indeed, it appears in the preface to *Milton: A Poem* (1804). Most famous for his epic poem *Paradise Lost*, Milton was also a Parliamentarian sympathizer who allied himself to Cromwell's new republic following the English Civil War. Inspired by the legend of Joseph of Arimathea's journey to England after the Crucifixion (**And did those feet in ancient times / Walk upon England's mountains green?**), he believed that by overthrowing their king, the English had been given the chance to build a new Jerusalem – a representation of heaven on earth.

Inspired by Milton's revolutionary story, Blake is in turn advocating further rebellion and change in his own time but in a **green and pleasant land** and not one scarred by factories belching smoke (**those dark satanic mills**). As a young man, the poet had witnessed with revulsion the development of the first mechanized steam-driven mill, the Albion Flour Mills, in 1786 at the beginning of the Industrial Revolution. The giant and noisy mill was so efficient it could have driven all the small windmills out of business had it not burned down only five years later, in 1791, under mysterious circumstances. In his poem, Blake is arguing that England has to reject industrialization and return to more basic Christian values.

But this interpretation – with its vision of heaven on earth – was completely ignored when the poem was included in a collection of patriotic verse, published in an effort to raise public morale when Britain was entrenched in the middle of the First World War. When C. Hubert H. Parry set the poem to music in 1916, 'Jerusalem' was immediately seen as defining exactly what Britain was fighting for. With its soldierly devotion to duty (**I will not cease from mental fight, / Nor shall my sword sleep in my hand**) and stirring melody, it has symbolized English patriotism ever since. Blake must be positively spinning in his grave. (For the biblical origins of **chariot of fire**, see SWING LOW, SWEET CHARIOT.)

# The Miller of Dee

THERE was a jolly miller once, lived on the river Dee;
He worked and sang from morn till night, no lark more blithe
    than he;
And this the burden of his song forever used to be:
'I care for nobody, no, not I, if nobody cares for me.'

The reason why he was so blithe, he once did thus unfold:
'The bread I eat my hands have earned, I covet no man's
    gold;
I do not fear next quarter-day, in debt to none I be;
I care for nobody, no, not I, if nobody cares for me.

'A coin or two I've in my purse, to help a needy friend,
A little I can give the poor and still have some to spend;
Though I may fail, yet I rejoice, another's good hap to see;
I care for nobody, no, not I, if nobody cares for me.'

So let us his example take and be from malice free,
Let every one his neighbour serve, as served he'd like to be
And merrily push the can about and drink and sing with glee:
'If nobody cares a doit for us, why not a doit care we.'

A traditional and popular English folksong from Cheshire,
'The Miller of Dee' has appeared in various forms, the
earliest of which was published in 1716. The Dee runs
through Chester, in Cheshire, and it is thought that the mill

of the song could have been one of many along the banks of the river near the town.

On the face of it, this song seems to be about self-sufficiency and happiness with your lot (**The bread I eat my hands have earned, I covet no man's gold**), embodied by the cheerful miller, who is presented as an inspiring example to all. However, a darker element can be discerned in the refrain: **I care for nobody, no, not I, if nobody cares for me.** The miller, ready to **help a needy friend** and **give to the poor,** appears otherwise to be driven purely by self-interest, detached from the community around him. Reaching the final verse, it seems that his example is actually only meant to inspire you to get drunk and ignore everyone who disagrees with you: **If nobody cares a doit for us, why not a doit care we.** And we all know what that is like, don't we!

Later versions of the song have tried to edit out this disturbing ambiguity, crafting the words into a much clearer moral message. Here the Scottish poet and songwriter Charles Mackay (1814–89) has removed all mention of money and alcohol and turned the song into a dialogue between the exemplary miller and an admiring King Hal (Henry VIII):

> There dwelt a miller hale and bold
> Beside the river Dee;
> He worked and sang from morn till night,
> No lark more blithe than he;
> And this the burden of his song
> Forever used to be, –

'I envy nobody; no, not I,
And nobody envies me!'

'Thou'rt wrong, my friend!' said good King Hal;
'Thou'rt wrong as wrong can be;
For could my heart be light as thine,
I'd gladly change with thee.
And tell me now, what makes thee sing,
With voice so loud and free,
While I am sad, though I'm the king,
Beside the river Dee.'

The miller smiled and doffed his cap:
'I earn my bread,' quoth he;
'I love my wife, I love my friend,
I love my children three;
I owe no penny I cannot pay;
I thank the river Dee,
That turns the mill that grinds the corn,
To feed my babes and me.'

'Good friend,' said Hal, and sighed the while,
'Farewell! and happy be;
But say no more, if thou'dst be true,
That no one envies thee.
Thy mealy cap is worth my crown,
Thy mill my kingdom's fee;
Such men as thou are England's boast,
O miller of the Dee!'

# The Skye Boat Song

SPEED, bonnie boat, like a bird on the wing,
Onward! the sailors cry;
Carry the bairn that's born to be king,
Over the sea to Skye.

Loud the winds howl, loud the waves roar,
Thunderclaps rend the air;
Baffled, our foes stand by the shore;
Follow, they will not dare.

Though the waves leap, soft shall ye sleep,
Ocean's a royal bed;
Rocked in the deep, Flora will keep
Watch by your weary head.

Many's the bairn fought on that day,
Well the claymore could wield;
When the night came, silently lay
Dead in Culloden's field.

Burned are their homes, exile and death
Scatter the loyal men;
Yet e'er the sword cool in the sheath,
Charlie will come again.

This moving song tells the tale of one of the famous stories of Scottish history, the escape of Bonnie Prince Charlie (**the bairn that's born to be king**) from the Duke of Cumberland's redcoats after the Battle of Culloden in 1746. The battle was a complete disaster for the Scots, and a large part of the responsibility rested with Charles's wrong-headed decisions on the battlefield (see THE LION AND THE UNICORN). Fleeing from the scene, Charles concluded that he had been betrayed and promptly abandoned the Jacobite cause, desperate to save his own skin. Despite a £30,000 reward for his capture, the Young Pretender survived for five months on the run in Scotland, protected and housed by his many supporters, at great personal risk to themselves.

The song tells the dramatic if humiliating story of the final stage of his escape from Scotland, disguised as a 'lady's maid' and posing as Betty Burke, maid to 24-year-old **Flora** MacDonald, who was later imprisoned in the Tower of London for her part in his escape. Charles returned to Italy the following year where he lived in Rome, drinking heavily and fathering numerous illegitimate children, until his death in 1788. (For the less glamorous side of the Jacobite rebellion, see ELSIE MARLEY.)

Many have assumed that the song is a traditional Scottish one, and the tune is an ancient Gaelic rowing song, but in fact the lyrics were written in 1884, by Sir Harold Boulton (1859–1935), although the melody could be based on a traditional one. The song was part of the Victorian obsession with the more picturesque moments in Scottish history, as spearheaded by Sir Walter Scott. An obvious clue to this is contained in its airbrushing of the less heroic parts of the escape: the fact that Charlie was desperately saving his own skin, leaving his men and everyone who had helped shelter him to be butchered, not to mention the ignominy of sneaking away dressed as a girl.

# The Star-Spangled Banner

OH, say can you see, by the dawn's early light,
What so proudly we hailed, at the twilight's last gleaming,
Whose broad stripes and bright stars, through the perilous
       fight,
O'er the ramparts we watched, were so gallantly streaming?
And the rockets' red glare, the bombs bursting in air,
Gave proof through the night that our flag was still there.
Oh, say, does that star-spangled banner yet wave
O'er the land of the free and the home of the brave?

This is the national anthem of the self-styled greatest nation on the planet and one of the better-known tunes in the world, the lyrics bursting with national pride and staunch heroism in the face of danger. Which is why it will please my Irish friends in Chicago no end when they find out that 'The Star-Spangled Banner' started out as a drinking song in eighteenth-century London. That should warm up a few baseball games down at the Hidden Shamrock, now that they know that.

The Anacreontic Society was a gentlemen's club formed in London during the mid 1700s, by a group of amateur musicians attempting to promote their craft – in honour of the Greek poet Anacreon (570–485 BC). The membership was known for its 'wit, harmony and love of wine'. The president of the Anacreontic Society, Ralph Tomlinson (1744–78), wrote the words to a drinking song that he called 'The Anacreontic Song' and which was soon adopted as the society's official anthem. The first verse goes like this:

> To Anacreon in heaven where he sat in full glee,
> A few sons of harmony sent in a petition,
> That he their inspirer and patron would be;
> When this answer arrived from the jolly old Grecian:,
> 'Voice, fiddle and flute, no longer be mute,
> I'll lend you my name and inspire you to boot.
> And besides, I'll instruct you like me to entwine
> The myrtle of Venus with Bacchus' wine.'

And so on it went for five more verses, each one encouraging the members to drink more heartily. The following year, a teenage composer and organist called John Stafford Smith (1750–1836) wrote the tune (now known as 'The Star-Spangled Banner') to fit Tomlinson's words and the popular song was first published in 1778. The raucous lyrics and memorable tune were soon well known throughout both England and America, with various tweaks to the words, especially in America where the resulting composition was used as a patriotic song under the titles 'Jefferson and Liberty' or 'Adams and Liberty'.

Over forty years later, on the night of 12 September 1814, an American attorney and poet, Francis Scott Key (1779–1843), was held prisoner on a British ship during the Battle of Baltimore. All night, British forces bombarded the town as one thousand committed Americans put up a stout defence despite their low numbers, and the following morning (**by the dawn's early light**) Scott was amazed and inspired to see the American flag still fluttering over Fort McHenry. With that, he sat down and rewrote 'The Anacreontic Song' with the words now associated with 'The Star-Spangled Banner'.

On 27 July 1889, the Secretary of the US Navy ordered that the song should be played every time the American flag was raised on any ship, and in 1916, as America entered the First World War, President Woodrow Wilson insisted the tune be heard at every military occasion. This soon extended to sporting occasions – within a few years, the baseball World Series was playing the song before every match. Then, on 3 March 1931, President Herbert Hoover passed a law adopting 'The Star-Spangled Banner' as the official national anthem of America. And, with that, a London drinking song had completed its chequered journey from dockside pub to the White House.

# Swing Low, Sweet Chariot

SWING low, sweet chariot,
Coming for to carry me home;
Swing low, sweet chariot,
Coming for to carry me home.

I looked over Jordan and what did I see,
Coming for to carry me home,
A band of angels coming after me,
Coming for to carry me home.

Swing low, sweet chariot,
Coming for to carry me home;
Swing low, sweet chariot,
Coming for to carry me home.

This famous song, beloved of England rugby fans, was originally written in 1862 by Wallis Willis, a freed slave of the Choctaw Indians of Oklahoma State. The official story goes that one day, as he was working in the cotton fields at Doaksville, on the banks of the Red River, Willis, homesick for his previous home along the Mississippi, made up the words of 'Swing Low, Sweet Chariot' off the top of his head and began singing them. He then made up more verses over the years that followed. However, as with HERE WE GO ROUND THE MULBERRY BUSH, this is no straightforward working song.

Some believe that the story of the song is simply based on Wallis's dream that God would carry him away to heaven, like the prophet Elijah in the Old Testament. Elijah's dramatic departure from Earth comes immediately after the waters of the river Jordan part, providing him with a path across (**I looked over Jordan and what did I see, / Coming for to carry me home**), after which a chariot and horses of fire appear and, in a whirlwind, lift the prophet to heaven. (Incidentally, it has been suggested that this is the Old Testament's alien abduction story: the chariot of fire could easily be an eighth-century BC description of a UFO, but that's another story.)

Although there are definite references to the story of Elijah, these are being used as a smokescreen to obscure the real message of the song. Willis was not the simple song-writer he pretended to be. His lyrics are couched in the language and style of straightforward spirituals but they're full of hidden meaning. Another very popular song of his was 'Steal Away', which was sung quietly by slaves who intended to break for freedom, in the hope of attracting other workers along with them:

> Steal away, steal away,
> Steal away to Jesus;
> Steal away, steal away,
> I ain't got long to stay here.

Seen in this light, 'Swing Low, Sweet Chariot' might in fact be a coded message about one of the best-kept secrets of the nineteenth century – the Underground Railroad. This was an informal network of secret routes and safe houses used by black slaves in the United States to escape to freedom with the aid of the abolitionists who were sympathetic to their cause. It was initially a network of routes from the Deep South to the northern states, but in 1850, after the Fugitive Slave Act allowed owners to pursue and recapture runaway slaves through the northern states of the Union, the Underground Railroad was extended to the Canadian border.

Support came from the African Methodist Episcopal Church, the African Baptist Church, the Scottish Presbyterian movement and the Quakers, who all provided food and shelter along the way, at great risk to themselves. The network was known as a 'railroad' because of its use of coded messages based on railway terminology. Individuals were often organized into small, independent groups, with little knowledge of each other beyond sister groups and connecting routes in the vicinity, which helped to maintain secrecy. The resting spots where the runaways could sleep and eat were given the code names 'stations' and 'depots', which were held by 'station masters'. There were also the 'conductors' who moved the runaways from station to station. These were often freed slaves from the North risking their own safety and liberty.

There are all kinds of colourful stories about how the coded messages were transmitted securely. It was too dangerous to write anything down and, besides, not all of the slaves were literate. Unusual and unexpected methods had to be employed. One theory is that fugitives were given quilts (primarily for bedding) whose designs provided coded maps to help direct them to stations. But an easier way was through song.

Many spirituals and other songs of the time contain information intended to help escaped slaves navigate the Railroad. One famous example is 'Follow the Drinking Gourd':

> When the sun comes back and the first quail calls,
> Follow the Drinkin' Gourd;
> For the old man's waitin' for to carry you to freedom
> If you follow the Drinkin' Gourd.

This song's message was to look to the skies. The constellation known as the Plough in Britain and the Big Dipper in North America was commonly called by its African name, the Drinking Gourd, by the slaves. The Drinking Gourd's 'bowl' points towards the North Star, hence the North and freedom.

'Swing Low, Sweet Chariot' therefore tells the story of a slave waiting to be shipped to freedom, calling on the Underground Railroad to **carry me home**. As if mimicking the way that the movement used the terminology of railways to disguise their actions, the song uses the archaic terminology of the Bible – after all, a **chariot** is about as near as the Old Testament gets to a railway train. As there are no angels in the story of Elijah, the **band of angels ... coming for to carry me home** could well be describing the religious organizations who were involved in the Railroad or even, as Canada and the North were already commonly referred to as the 'Promised Land', everyone who dwelt there already.

Another four verses take the story of the journey further. They hint at the perils of the journey (**Sometimes I'm up and sometimes I'm down**) and are full of motivating reminders of that new life ahead (**my soul feels heavenly bound ... Jesus washed my sins away**):

> Sometimes I'm up and sometimes I'm down,
> Coming for to carry me home;
> But still my soul feels heavenly bound,
> Coming for to carry me home.
>
> The brightest day that I can say,
> Coming for to carry me home,
> When Jesus washed my sins away,
> Coming for to carry me home.
>
> If I get there before you do,
> Coming for to carry me home,
> I'll cut a hole and pull you through,
> Coming for to carry me home.
>
> If you get there before I do,
> Coming for to carry me home,
> Tell all my friends I'm coming too,
> Coming for to carry me home.

The penultimate verse makes a promise that the singer will physically come back and help those who remain behind (**If I get there before you do ... I'll cut a hole and pull you**

**through**), as the slave audience would know that most of the 'conductors' on the Underground Railroad were former slaves, like Wallis Willis himself. The final verse is all about the importance of spreading the message of hope to all those slaves who weren't yet on their way to freedom (**Tell all my friends I'm coming**). The Underground Railroad would make sure they were all eventually freed.

## Yankee Doodle Dandy

YANKEE Doodle went to town
A-riding on a pony;
He stuck a feather in his hat
And called it macaroni.

Yankee Doodle, keep it up,
Yankee Doodle dandy;
Mind the music and the step
And with the girls be handy.

Set rather incongruously to the tune of an English rhyme about prostitution (see LUCY LOCKET), 'Yankee Doodle Dandy', now the official anthem of Connecticut, was made up by British army officers in the late 1700s to mock their indisciplined and dishevelled Yankee counterparts during the French and Indian War (1754–63; part of the Seven Years' War between Britain and France). **Doodle** is a slang word for a simpleton or village idiot, while a **macaroni** (from the Italian *maccherone* or 'boorish fool') was the term for a fop or man obsessed with fashion. Hence fun is being poked at this simple fellow who thinks he's the very height of fashion for just sticking a **feather in his hat**.

The song also made the term **Yankee** more widely known. Thought to have derived from the Cherokee Indian word for 'coward', *eankke*, it was originally used to describe Dutch settlers in New England, evolving into a derogatory term for the would-be American citizens during the settlers' battle for independence from the British Crown in 1775–83.

# Sources and Further Reading

*Curious Myths of the Middle Ages* (1868 and 1870) by
   Sabine Baring-Gould
*Brewer's Dictionary of Phrase and Fable* (2001 edition)
*The Origins of English Nonsense* (1997) by Noel Malcolm
*Dictionary of Celtic Mythology* (1998) by James
   MacKillop
*The English Year* (2005) by Steve Roud
*Dickens* (1990) and *London* (2000) by Peter Ackroyd
*The Lore of the Land* (2004) by Jennifer Westwood and
   Jacqueline Simpson
*The Uses of Enchantment: The Meaning and Importance
   of Fairy Tales* (1976) by Bruno Bettelheim
*Alice's Adventures in Wonderland* (1865) and *Through the
   Looking-Glass, and What Alice Found There* (1871) by
   Lewis Carroll
*A Book of Nonsense and More Nonsense* (1862) by
   Edward Lear

And then, there are various books about nursery rhymes. As I said in the Introduction, I don't agree with all their arguments but they definitely make for interesting reading ...

*The Oxford Dictionary of Nursery Rhymes* (1951) by Iona
   and Peter Opie

*The Oxford Nursery Rhyme Book* (1963) by Iona and
   Peter Opie
*Nursery Rhymes and Tales, Their Origin and History*
   (1924) by Henry Bett
*The Plague and the Fire* (1961) by James Leasor
*Heavy Words, Lightly Thrown* (2003) by Chris Roberts

# Index

# ANNE FADIMAN

---

**EX LIBRIS**
ANNE FADIMAN

'Witty, enchanting and supremely well written' Robert McCrum, *Observer*

This witty collection of essays recounts a lifelong love affair with books and language. For Fadiman, as for many passionate readers, the books she loves have become chapters in her own life story.

Writing with remarkable grace, she revives the tradition of the well-crafted personal essay, moving easily from anecdotes about Coleridge and Orwell to tales of her own pathologically literary family. As someone who played at blocks with her father's 22-volume set of Trollope ('My Ancestral Castles') and who only really considered herself married when she and her husband had merged collections ('Marrying Libraries'), she is exquisitely well equipped to expand upon the art of inscriptions, the perverse pleasures of compulsive proof-reading, the allure of long words, and the satisfactions of reading out loud. There is even a foray into pure literary gluttony – Charles Lamb liked buttered muffin crumbs between the leaves, and Fadiman knows of more than one reader who literally consumes page corners.

Perfectly balanced between humour and erudition, *Ex Libris* establishes Fadiman as one of the world's finest contemporary essayists.

'*Ex Libris* will provide enjoyable moments of recognition for all book obsessives'
Alain de Botton

---

# PARTICULAR BOOKS

**THE OLD DOG AND DUCK:**
**THE SECRET MEANINGS OF PUB NAMES**
ALBERT JACK

This is a book for everyone who has ever wondered why pubs should be called
The Cross Keys, The Dew Drop Inn or The Hope and Anchor. You'll be glad to
know that there are very good – strange and memorable – reasons behind them
all, showing that, ultimately, the story of pub history is really the story of our own
popular history

After much research about (and in) pubs, Albert Jack brings together the stories
behind pub names to reveal how they offer fascinating and subversive insights on
our history, customs, attitudes and jokes in just the same way that nursery rhymes
do. The Royal Oak, for instance, commemorates the tree that hid Charles II from
Cromwell's forces after his defeat at Worcester; The Bag of Nails is a corruption of
the Bacchanals, the crazed followers of Bacchus, the god of wine and drunkenness;
The Cat and the Fiddle a mangling of Catherine La Fidele and a guarded gesture
of support for Henry VIII's first, Catholic, wife Catherine of Aragon; plus many,
many more.

'The man with the answers is Albert Jack' *Daily Express*

# PARTICULAR BOOKS

**WHY IS Q ALWAYS FOLLOWED BY U?**
MICHAEL QUINION

Long-time word-detective and bestselling author of *Port Out, Starboard Home*, Michael Quinion brings us the answers to nearly two hundred of the most intriguing questions he's been asked about language over the years. Sent to him by enquiring readers from all around the globe, Michael's answers about the meanings and histories behind the quirky phrases, slang and language that we all use are set to delight, amuse and enlighten even the most hardened word-obsessive.

• Did you know that 'Blighty' comes from an ancient Arabic word?

• Or that Liberace cried his way to the bank so many times people think he came up with the phrase?

• That 'cloud nine' started out as 'cloud seven' in the speakeasies of '30s America?

• And that the first person to have their thunder stolen was a dismal playwright from Drury Lane?

*Why is Q Always Followed By U?* is full of surprising discoveries, entertaining quotations and memorable information. Michael Quinion will help you discover the truth that lies behind the *cock-and-bull* stories and make sure you're always linguistically *on the ball*.

'Quinion brilliantly tackles the riddles of so many of the sayings we've long puzzled over: he's authoritative, quirky, and always entertaining' Susie Dent

# PENGUIN HUMOUR

**SHAGGY DOGS & BLACK SHEEP**
ALBERT JACK

The English language is crammed with colourful phrases and sayings that we use without thinking every day. It's only when we're asked who *smart Alec* or *Holy Moly* were, where feeling *in the pink* or *once in a blue moon* come from that we realize that there's far more to English than we might have thought.

Luckily enough, we have Albert Jack, who has explored the origins of hundreds of phrases from around the world. The fascinating stories he has uncovered come from the rich traditions of the navy, army and law to confidence tricksters and highwaymen, from the practices of ancient civilizations to Music Hall and pubs.

*Shaggy Dogs and Black Sheep* is a compulsively readable, highly enlightening look at the phrases we use all the time but rarely consider. From the skin of your teeth to the graveyard shift – you'll never speak (or even think) English in the same way again.

'Just "the bees knees" . . . you'll never think of English in the same way again'
*Irish Times*

# PENGUIN HUMOUR

## LOCH NESS MONSTERS AND RAINING FROGS

ALBERT JACK

In *Loch Ness Monsters and Raining Frogs* the world's strangest questions are answered: What happened to the *Mary Celeste*? Where is the Mona Lisa? (clue: it's not in the Louvre). Is the Loch Ness Monster really a circus elephant? Will the real Paul McCartney please stand up? Who killed Marilyn Monroe? What was Agatha Christie's own mystery? Why does it rain frogs? Does Bigfoot exist? How did D. B Cooper get away with the perfect crime? (To name but some).

With enough entertaining information to fuel hundreds of pub conversations, fascinating illustrations and all kinds of discoveries to surprise even the most expert conspiracy theorist, *Loch Ness Monsters and Raining Frogs* is the perfect present for anybody who's ever wondered why …

'From the Bermuda Triangle to the Loch Ness Monster, Albert Jack offers a crash-course in sceptical thinking' *Independent*, Books of the Year

# PENGUIN HUMOUR

**PHANTOM HITCHHIKERS AND DECOY DUCKS**

ALBERT JACK

Conspiracies, alien landings and missing kidneys ... Albert Jack goes sleuthing in the mysterious realm of urban legends.

From Walt Disney's frozen head to the kidnap of JFK's brain, Albert Jack gathers together all the strangest, sickest, funniest and most unforgettable urban legends and recounts them with his usual deadpan humour. But this is more than just a collection of urban legends, it is also a detective story. Exploring the real events behind conspiracy theories, the exaggerations of history and the assumptions of old wives' tales, Albert Jack shows us that the truth can definitely be stranger than fiction ...

'The man with the answers is Albert Jack' *Daily Express*

# He just wanted a decent book to read ...

Not too much to ask, is it? It was in 1935 when Allen Lane, Managing Director of Bodley Head Publishers, stood on a platform at Exeter railway station looking for something good to read on his journey back to London. His choice was limited to popular magazines and poor-quality paperbacks – the same choice faced every day by the vast majority of readers, few of whom could afford hardbacks. Lane's disappointment and subsequent anger at the range of books generally available led him to found a company – and change the world.

*'We believed in the existence in this country of a vast reading public for intelligent books at a low price, and staked everything on it'*
**Sir Allen Lane, 1902–1970, founder of Penguin Books**

The quality paperback had arrived – and not just in bookshops. Lane was adamant that his Penguins should appear in chain stores and tobacconists, and should cost no more than a packet of cigarettes.

Reading habits (and cigarette prices) have changed since 1935, but Penguin still believes in publishing the best books for everybody to enjoy. We still believe that good design costs no more than bad design, and we still believe that quality books published passionately and responsibly make the world a better place.

So wherever you see the little bird – whether it's on a piece of prize-winning literary fiction or a celebrity autobiography, political tour de force or historical masterpiece, a serial-killer thriller, reference book, world classic or a piece of pure escapism – you can bet that it represents the very best that the genre has to offer.

**Whatever you like to read – trust Penguin.**